TROUT MASK R

Praise for the

It was only a matter of time before a clever publisher realized that there is an audience for whom *Exile on Main Street* or *Electric Ladyland* are as significant and worthy of study as *The Catcher in the Rye* or *Middlemarch* … The series … is freewheeling and eclectic, ranging from minute rock-geek analysis to idiosyncratic personal celebration — *The New York Times Book Review*

Ideal for the rock geek who thinks liner notes just aren't enough — *Rolling Stone*

One of the coolest publishing imprints on the planet — *Bookslut*

These are for the insane collectors out there who appreciate fantastic design, well-executed thinking, and things that make your house look cool. Each volume in this series takes a seminal album and breaks it down in startling minutiae. We love these. We are huge nerds — *Vice*

A brilliant series … each one a work of real love — *NME* (UK)

Passionate, obsessive, and smart — *Nylon*

Religious tracts for the rock 'n' roll faithful — *Boldtype*

[A] consistently excellent series — *Uncut* (UK)

We … aren't naive enough to think that we're your only source for reading about music (but if we had our way … watch out). For those of you who really like to know everything there is to know about an album, you'd do well to check out Continuum's "33 1/3" series of books — *Pitchfork*

For reviews of individual titles in the series, please visit our blog at 333sound.com and our website at http://www.bloomsbury.com/musicandsoundstudies

Follow us on Twitter: @333books

Like us on Facebook: https://www.facebook.com/33.3books

For a complete list of books in this series, see the back of this book

For more information about the series, please visit our new blog:

www.333sound.com

Where you'll find:

– Author and artist interviews

– Author profiles

– News about the series

– How to submit a proposal to our open call

– Things we find amusing

Trout Mask Replica

Kevin Courrier

BLOOMSBURY ACADEMIC
NEW YORK • LONDON • OXFORD • NEW DELHI • SYDNEY

BLOOMSBURY ACADEMIC
Bloomsbury Publishing Inc
1385 Broadway, New York, NY 10018, USA
50 Bedford Square, London, WC1B 3DP, UK
29 Earlsfort Terrace, Dublin 2, Ireland

BLOOMSBURY, BLOOMSBURY ACADEMIC and the Diana logo are trademarks of
Bloomsbury Publishing Plc

First published in Great Britain 2007 by the Continuum International Publishing Group Ltd
Reprinted 2012
Reprinted by Bloomsbury Academic 2013
Reprinted 2014, 2016, 2017, 2018 (twice), 2019, 2021, 2022, 2023, 2024

Library of Congress Cataloging-in-Publication Data
Courrier, Kevin, 1954-
Trout mask replica / by Kevin Courrier.
p. cm. – (33 1/3)
ISBN-13: 978-0-8264-2781-6 (pbk.: alk. paper)
ISBN-10: 0-8264-2781-2 (pbk.: alk. paper)
1. Captain Beefheart. Trout mask replica. 2. Rock
music–1961-1970–
History and criticism. I. Title. II. Series.
ML420.C2535C68 2007
782.421660092–dc22
2007002716

ISBN: PB: 978-0-8264-2781-6
ePDF: 978-1-4411-1377-1
eBook: 978-1-4411-9269-1

Series: 33 1/3, volume 44

Printed and bound in Great Britain

To find out more about our authors and books visit www.bloomsbury.com and
sign up for our newsletters.

Contents

Acknowledgments

Although this was the most enjoyable (and least disruptive) experience I've had yet writing a book, the idea for this little tome followed some rather unfortunate circumstances. After working as a film critic at the Canadian Broadcasting Corporation for close to fifteen years, I was let go in 2005 by an aspiring executive who didn't find me (among other things) consumer-friendly enough. It therefore seemed perfectly fitting to go on to write a book about an album that was even less consumer-friendly than me.

For that, I have to offer deep thanks to David Barker, my editor at Continuum press, for giving me the opportunity to delve deeply—but quickly—into my love for a peculiar record that makes demands on that love. Besides being the progenitor of a fascinating series of books for those who truly adore music, David continues to affirm my faith that there are still sharp editors dedicated to creating a nurturing climate for good writing. (He also returns every e-mail query promptly.)

Gabriella Page-Fort supplied a concise copyedit, too, which made my job as a writer about as painless as anyone could hope for.

While writing is always a solitary act, I have a few readers to thank who made it less lonely. Shlomo Schwartzberg bravely tore through this text, and offered invaluable advice, even though he could barely stand to listen to two minutes of the actual album. Naomi Boxer was unflinchingly supportive, extremely helpful, and enormously generous in her comments. Besides being a great friend, John Corcelli offered some deeply insightful suggestions that cleared my head long enough to take the text further than I had planned. Adam Nayman, who is one of the brightest young film critics around, is also a cherished and deeply valued friend. Our endless conversations consistently opened up ideas that found there way into informing this book. David Churchill, one of my oldest and dearest friends, always asks the right questions and provides the best answers. Donald Brackett is every bit part of the fabric of this book. As with my previous efforts on Randy Newman and Frank Zappa, this one also grew out of long passionate discussions about music dating back to 1985.

There are some other special people to thank for the indispensable role they play (or have played) in my both my personal and professional life: Albert & Sheila Vezeau, Scott and Shawn Courrier, Steve Vineberg, Annie Bryant, Mimi Gellman, Dave King and Lynne Godfrey, Avril Orloff, Susan Green, Judith Edwards, Leonore Johnston, Lynne Teperman, Nick Power, Jean Jinnah, Brian Quinn & Vi, Mi-Kyong Shim, Bob Douglas and Gayle Burns, Larry Rooney, Jack David, Jen Hale, the late Tom Fulton, Dave Downey, Anton Leo, Janice

Newton, Sandra Kerr, and my special colleagues and friends at Public Outreach, who every day remind me of the value of professional integrity and dedicated idealism.

Special gratitude also goes to Mimi Divinsky, who truly made this book possible with her profuse generosity and precious friendship.

I set out to write this book with a keen ear for the larger culture that informs Beefheart's work, in an effort to prove that it doesn't exist in a vacuum. It's an important aspect of what a good critic does. For those fans on Internet sites, though, who only crave "new information" (i.e. minutiae), or resent other informed voices who value digging into the "nilly-willy" in order to get at the "nitty-gritty," this book may not satisfy any fetishistic urges. I can only paraphrase Frank Zappa: information is not knowledge. For those fans inquiring enough to delve into what is maybe (for you) a familiar story, I've tried to magnify my appraisal of one of America's most original artists by including those (like Blind Willie Johnson) who also occupy a kindred spirit of invention. In that vein, I hope you find this book an enjoyable and valuable edition to the ongoing discussion of *Trout Mask Replica*.

Kevin Courrier
February, 2007.

Preface
The Truth Has No Patterns

Like most stories, the tale of this particular book begins with an earlier one. It's about a love affair with music, and how our liaison with music takes unpredictable twists and turns. As our encounters in romance can begin so suddenly, so innocently, so mysteriously, timeless music can also follow a similar course. A record will sometimes hit us quite unexpectedly on a car radio, right at that moment when the music and the commercials blend into one totally innocuous whole. That's how I discovered Bob Dylan's "Like a Rolling Stone," for instance, on a family vacation to Florida. My father, who was driving the car (and who hated rock and roll), became so transfixed by the tidal pull of the song that even he couldn't find the will to change the station. Other times, it happens through chance encounters with an acquaintance.

When I first met Brian Potts in 1964—a grade school classmate I knew only from a distance—he adamantly insisted that I come over and listen to Beatles records at his house.

When I told him that I had no interest in listening to music by four obnoxiously cute British guys in similar suits and cereal-bowl haircuts, he played me "It Won't Be Long," which opened *With the Beatles* with thunderous joy. I immediately shut up. Brian and I became, for a few years, inseparable friends. Much later, we even shared Dylan's epic "Sad Eyed Lady of the Lowlands" from *Blonde on Blonde*. I remember both of us, wide-eyed twelve-year-olds, in dazed silence, trying to find suitable words to explain how such a poetically dense song could hold us for the whole side of an album. But that's generally how we come to discover the music we fall in love with: the serendipity of friendship. There are other times, though, when music has a way of discovering you rather than the other way around. Unlike most pop music, it can connect with you in such an immediate and startling way that you ultimately have to catch up to it. The encounter does more than simply defy your expectations—it renders them inadequate to the occasion. So it was with Captain Beefheart & the Magic Band's 1969 double-LP, *Trout Mask Replica*. As with the previously discovered records, it, too, was a friend who introduced me to it.

In 1972, I had been working at a Youth Centre in Oshawa, Ontario, Canada, a small industrial town where General Motors was the economic engine of the city. With very little cultural life going on and boredom always looming on the horizon, some kids just naturally turned to drugs. One of them was my friend Mike, a young speed dealer who sampled his own merchandise maybe a little too often. A few years earlier, Mike had lost part of his leg when, much to his horror, he couldn't outrun a moving train. Now hiding a partial limp, he moved through life as if he were still within earshot of that predatory caboose. One day, Mike came up to the Centre while I was on shift helping other youngsters find ways to get off drugs. It was pretty common for folks to just wander in and hang out and chat, while waiting to see what crisis might come through the door. Oddly enough, it was in this centre that Mike always seemed relaxed and friendly. Who knows? Maybe it was in this sanctuary that he felt no longer encumbered by his street identity as the speed dealer.

On this particular day, I was talking to a coworker about *Hot Rats*, a 1969 Frank Zappa album I had first heard a couple of summers earlier. I commented on how the record had opened up, for me, a world of fascinating sounds by providing a storehouse of musical technique. It was liberating, I suggested, to hear energetic music that so freely combined such vastly diverse styles. Suddenly, Mike piped up from across the room, "Have you ever heard *Trout Mask Replica*?" Others in the office chuckled, as if some joke were being cracked to challenge a title as ridiculous as *Hot Rats*. But I had actually heard of *Trout Mask*. In fact, I knew of Captain Beefheart. He sang the only song that wasn't an instrumental on *Hot Rats*, a blistering blues track called "Willie the Pimp." Under the searing melody of Sugarcane Harris's violin and fuelled by Zappa's blast furnace guitar, Beefheart introduced Willie with a deep growling snarl that suggested Howlin' Wolf on a midnight prowl. "I'm a little pimp with my hair gassed back," he announced with libidinal delight, "pair of khaki pants and my shoes shined black." It's a powerhouse performance, but it was a brief one, since the epic track was for the most part an instrumental showcase for Zappa's dexterous guitar work.

Although "Willie the Pimp" served as an overwhelming introduction to Beefheart's limitless power as a blues singer, I was familiar with little else about him. A few months earlier, I had purchased a record called *Zapped*, a sampler anthology that Zappa's record company had released featuring a number of artists signed to his Bizarre/Straight label. On this album, among tracks by Alice Cooper; a schizophrenic street busker named Wild Man Fischer; fifties hipster poet Lord Buckley; folkies Tim Buckley, Jerry Yester, and Judy Henske; the GTO's (a female groupie band); plus Zappa's own Mothers of Invention were two songs by Captain Beefheart ("The Blimp (mousetrapreplica)" and "Old Fart at Play") from *Trout Mask Replica*.

Upon reading the liner notes on *Zapped*, I saw that Zappa had actually produced *Trout Mask*. "The Blimp (mousetrap-replica)" was a frenzied poetic recitation by a member of Beefheart's Magic Band and recorded by Zappa over the telephone in the studio. He layered this delirious reading simultaneously overtop a repetitive bed of abstract jazz by the Mothers. "The Blimp" was a hilariously wild yarn of sexual terror cast in the famous soundscape of the Hindenberg disaster broadcast:

> All the people stir
> 'n the girl's knees tremble
> 'n run their hands over the blimp, the blimp.

By contrast, "Old Fart at Play" had Beefheart himself reading a luxuriantly textured sensual limerick:

> Her stockings down caught dust 'n doughballs
> She cracked 'er mouth glaze caught one eyelash
> Rubbed 'er hands on 'er gorgeous gingham.

For over its two-minute length, the song evolved into an intangible story of a man being reborn in a "wooden fish-head." Since the track was sandwiched between "Lucille Has Messed My Mind Up," a straightforward R&B performance by ex-Mother Jeff Simmons (with Zappa providing some tasty blues licks on the guitar), and the Mothers' own Kurt Weill–flavoured "Holiday in Berlin, Full Blown," "Old Fart at Play" seemed more a musical segue on *Zapped* than a clue to what secrets *Trout Mask Replica* actually held.

In answer to Mike's question, I told him that I knew a couple of tracks from the record, but that was it. He persevered, "Yeah, but have you heard the whole album?" I pleaded ignorance. "No. I haven't even seen it, Mike," I replied. "Well, I've got it," he said as if he'd just revealed ownership of the Maltese Falcon. Being both curious and excited, I asked him if I could borrow it. "Borrow it?" he asked incredulously. "You can *have* it!" All eyes in the room suddenly looked to Mike as if he were privy to a long dark secret we all wanted in on. "I can't listen to it, Courrier," he said wincing at the very thought of hearing it. "It's a horrible record! Noise, just nothing but noise. It makes me . . . nervous." After a man has lost part of his leg to a moving train, one begins to quickly wonder what kind of music could possibly make him "nervous." But I accepted his offer and took *Trout Mask Replica* off his hands.

When Mike delivered the record, I realized that I first needed to get past the front cover before I could ever come close to sampling the music. Some of Zappa's album covers had been intimidating, too, but they were also so oddly amusing, so deliberately poking fun, that they became ultimately approachable. The front cover of *Trout Mask Replica* didn't

seem funny at all. It was earnest rather than satirical. It exud-
ed a quiet comfort about its own weirdness which just added
to my discomfort looking at it. The back cover (featuring the
refurbished Magic Band in their exotic apparel) merely confirmed my fears of what a hippie commune would look like
once it had gone to seed. Their names were stranger than
their looks. Someone named Zoot Horn Rollo was on glass-
finger guitar and flute. I would later discover he was a young
blues guitarist named Bill Harkleroad. ("Contrary to what was
written on *Trout Mask Replica*, I never played flute with the
band," Harkleroad asserts today.) Antennae Jimmy Semens,
who turned out to be Harkleroad's friend Jeff Cotton, was
listed as playing a steel-appendage guitar. The Mascara Snake,
who was Beefheart's cousin and also a painter, played bass
clarinet and sang. ("He couldn't play a lick but had a lot of
attitude," Harkleroad adds.) The bass player had the oddly
quirky name of Rockette Morton (Beefheart: "What do you
run on Rockette Morton? Say beans." Morton: "I run on
beans. I run on laser beans"). He turned out to be Mark
Boston, another musical pal of Harkleroad's. Oddly, there was
no drummer credited. You certainly heard one once you
played this record. There wasn't anyone—anywhere—who
got sounds like these from his drum kit. In time, I discovered
his name was John French (who had earned the appropriate
moniker Drumbo, a Disney pun), and he turned out to be a
pivotal figure in the making of this music. Although uncred-
ited in the liner notes, French is featured on the back cover
lurking under the bridge beneath the rest of the band. So why
was he was airbrushed (momentarily) out of history? It took
years to find out.

On the front, there was Beefheart in a green coat lined

with dirty white fur hanging limply around his neck. It resembled some malnourished fox that had taken rest there many years earlier (and since died). Beefheart wore a huge stovepipe hat on his head, with a swizzle bulb on the top, as if he were the Grand Wazoo of some rogue band of Shriners. Covering his face was a real trout mask, with its eyes glaring out into the great beyond. Its open mouth was framed by an elegant thread-thin moustache, while Beefheart's hand, holding the trout mask in place, was open-palmed. His pose suggested he was casually waving to someone across the street. The music? There was nothing casual about that.

On the opening track, "Frownland," I heard an urgent manifesto, one boldly declaring a new world and a new music. Off the mark, Beefheart states defiantly that his spirit is in harmony with the natural world. He'd never go back to "yer Frownland." Yet the music that surrounds him is anything but harmonious. The sound seems to come from some hidden gulag *in* Frownland. The charging guitar chords that begin the tune are as recognizably insolent as the ones that open "(I Can't Get No) Satisfaction." But the moment Beefheart declares that his "smile is stuck," the rhythms clash and collide around that paralysed grin like a collection of rocks crumbling down in a mountain avalanche. You're forced to think: If this man is happy, what can Frownland possibly be like? "With that voice, he sounds like he's been a resident in Frownland his whole life," a friend suggested years later. There is an open paradox in the song revealing to listeners a romantic who doesn't feel part of a harmonious landscape. Of course, that puts him in good company with a number of American musical artists—from Charles Ives to Harry Partch —who defined their work by boldly sparring with the young and turbulent country that spawned them. Yet with Beefheart, the rancour doesn't seem driven by a need to sound different. It resembles the declarations of a man who was different because it was the only way he could truly be himself.

As a listening experience, *Trout Mask Replica* is the story of an artist who finds himself at his most free. It is a tale of one who refuses the comforts of security, yet still continues to dream of a world where man and beast can commingle in harmony. In staking that territory, from a musical standpoint, Beefheart doesn't rely on the lovely pop hooks that we ache to hear as listeners. The freedom *Trout Mask* offers is freedom from the familiar—the very element that often makes an album a hit, or at least, an audience favorite.

Despite the abrasive atonality of the music, the varied themes on *Trout Mask* are never less than inviting. Whether it's the pure erotic sensuality of the passionate wet sex in "Neon Meate Dream of a Octafish"; or the abstract a cappella recitation of "The Dust Blows Forward 'n the Dust Blows Back," which seems to conjure up a Walt Whitman poem after it has been soaked in hillbilly booze; or "Dachau Blues," where the horror of the Holocaust gets dipped in an abstract rendering of apocalyptic gospel, Beefheart openly welcomes listeners to hear him rail against a world that is often at odds with his own distinct brand of humanism. The unsettling nature of the songs somehow guarantees a more hermetic audience for this album. Beefheart defined that sensibility years later as "music from the other side of the fence." By drawing that line in the sand, he continually puts his audience to the test in trying to define exactly how that fence separates his music from all others'. Elvis, the Beatles, the Stones, they all reached out with their best songs to create a larger popular appeal, a culture that would share the pleasures held within their music. Beefheart, on *Trout Mask*, assures us that those pleasures could only be reaped in isolation. His was not a party album—unless you wanted the party to go home.

If *Trout Mask* is to be considered a hermetic experience, it ultimately inherited a secret society of followers consistently keeping its spirit alive. Unfortunately, the same couldn't be said for Mike. After he divested himself of the record, he just couldn't find solace in anything else. Within a few weeks of my receiving *Trout Mask*, Mike committed suicide. His death continues to overshadow my listening to the record, not only because the record had once spooked him, but because *Trout Mask Replica* became a parting gift before I could ever tell him my thoughts about it. Lost was an opportunity to remove his burden of being "nervous" about its contents. But stories never do end so simply.

As it turns out, I didn't have to consider my possession of *Trout Mask* for long. Just before the funeral, his mother came to visit me at my apartment looking for items he may have recently lent to his friends. "I'd like to bury him with some of his favourite things," she told me. Maybe if I had kept my mouth shut, I might still own that original first pressing of *Trout Mask Replica* on Straight Records, and he wouldn't have literally taken it to his grave. But while telling her about this strange record, she immediately assumed that I was lying about being the new owner and wanted the album back. How could I argue with a grieving mother? I reluctantly gave it to her and never saw her again. I didn't buy another copy until Halloween night in 1987.

On that evening, I was going out on a second date with a woman I recently met. There I was dressed in a powder blue suit with a wicked cat's face painted on my face, and we were off to see Clive Barker's movie *Hellraiser* in preparation for a radio interview I was doing with him a few days later. Before arriving for the special screening at the Bloor Cinema in Toronto, I detoured into Peter Dunn's Vinyl Museum to look for records. While combing through the stacks, grinning through my painted whiskers at curious onlookers, I found a brand new sealed copy of *Trout Mask Replica* on Reprise Records. Without thinking, I immediately snapped it up and ran to the counter. As the clerk was ringing it up, I started thinking of Mike, fifteen years in his grave, helplessly cradling the very record that had once so unnerved him. That night, masked and disguised, as Beefheart was himself on the cover, I had once again inherited this album. Mike and I now both possessed it. But I was to go forward into the years ahead, continuing to plumb the bottomless mysteries of this odd epic masterpiece. The very friend who introduced me to it lay motionless, somewhere deep in a hole in Oshawa, still being chased by the music he couldn't escape.

This book is for him.

Chapter One
A Desert Island of the Mind

Everybody hears my music, but the thing is, it's a matter of whether they want to or not. I don't know how
people can say they don't hear . . . like that [car] horn,
when that horn is there. That's what gets me. What
the hell are they doing, man? What are they doing? I
mean, people must know they're wrong. They must
know some of the things they're doing are so far back
that a train don't go there.

—Don Van Vliet, "Captain Beefheart
Pulls a Hat Out of His Rabbit"

Trout Mask Replica is an album so assured in its isolated world-
view that no matter how much it might alienate potential listeners, it still demands to be heard—on its own terms. Yet
unlike most commercial pop, Beefheart doesn't write songs to
seduce an audience. We're not asked to identify with him in

this music because his songs aren't a conventional baring of the artist's soul. Beefheart invites us to experience *Trout Mask Replica*, rather than telling us what to experience. So whoever you choose to share this strident and peculiar record with, you're always going to be on your own with it. Which is why *Trout Mask Replica* embodied the punk aesthetic eight years before it exploded in the UK with the Sex Pistols. If the 60s hippie culture was clannish, punks were solitary. "Punks were self-consciously outsiders in school and at work," critic Greil Marcus told Geoff Pevere of the Canadian Broadcasting Corporation. "They picked things to like that nobody else did. They dressed differently, talked differently, and they weren't joiners." *Trout Mask* would quite naturally inspire countless other artists—from the Clash to P.J. Harvey—in finding their own sound, their own voice—to walk comfortably alone in the world. "If you listen to it, you will find a world of voices speaking to you from all directions," Marcus explained. "You might feel both exhilarated and completely lost." Perhaps it was this very quality of being lost that made Mike feel so "nervous" about *Trout Mask*. The record didn't provide a map to guide him in finding his way back into the larger world again, the way most great pop music can. This album was about discovering yourself as an alien, about being as different as Mike once felt minus part of his leg. Beefheart's utopia wasn't borne out of the real world, a world that Mike had wished himself to be part of again. Beefheart's utopia is the true definition of the word—nowhere—a desert island of the mind.

Curiously, a few years after Mike handed me the *Trout Mask Replica* album, the record became part of a particular desert island study among music critics: What album would you take with you if you were isolated on a desert island? It's always been a tempting question, essentially a popular party staple which allows music critics a casual forum to defend their tastes, test the wits of others, plus brag about rare records that nobody but them gives a damn about. The idea is also a bit ridiculous. (What critic would ever want to be isolated on a desert island with no access to concerts, free CDs, records, or even an outlet to express his or her persuasive views?) After all, isn't music, even in the current age of iPods, still best enjoyed in a communal environment? A desert island seems to negate the whole purpose of music. It denies music an audience, save for that one lone fan, to test its true value. Yet this question became the subject of a 1979 book called *Stranded: Rock and Roll for a Desert Island*, in which twenty prominent American rock critics were asked by fellow scribe Greil Marcus to contribute an essay in response to this curious (and appetizing) request.

The concept of the desert island was intended to be a purely metaphorical one. But was it? In his introduction to *Stranded*, Marcus comments, "When I began to call up people I thought would be interested and asked them that question, asked them to contribute, the response was enthusiastic, but in many cases for a reason I hadn't anticipated. 'A great idea,' said one person after another. 'I feel like I've been living on a desert island for years.'" A remark like that can lead a reader to think that, included in *Stranded*, there will be essays about music that can only be nurtured in isolation, in the mind and tastes of the writer. Upon looking through some of the selections, though, the desert island records invited more of a crowd than many of these writers thought. For example, Simon Frith, a former columnist for *Creem* and *Melody Maker*, decided to bring along *Beggar's Banquet* (1968), the Rolling

Stones' exquisitely popular tribute to country blues—hardly a record you could imagine wanting to hear alone. M. Mark, the former arts editor of the *Village Voice*, provided a fascinating overview of the mystically dark Celtic poetry of Van Morrison. This brooding Belfast Cowboy with his wailing brogue certainly wasn't a voice made for a desert island. The late Lester Bangs, who described how Morrison's *Astral Weeks* (1968) actually pulled him *out* of the painful isolation of a horrible year, makes the opposite argument of the book.

Most of the artists cited—whether it was Tom Smucker on the glorious gospel recordings of Thomas A. Dorsey or Kit Rachlis on the hauntingly lonely sound of Neil Young's voice—were people that ultimately did reach (and intended to reach) a larger audience. Even if their work originated from a private, sometimes isolated pain (like Young), their records continued to exist because their purpose was to create a bridge from those desert islands to a broader civilization— where anxious ears were yearning to listen to them. Most of the essays were private musings by intelligent critics eloquently championing their favorite music. (Since he was the editor, Greil Marcus actually got to cheat and bring most of his own record collection to the island.)

The only essay in the book that, for me, made a convincing argument was Langdon Winner's on *Trout Mask Replica*. Winner, formerly a political theorist, had written extensively about rock and roll for a variety of music magazines. He instinctively knew that this record was not one that was shaped for popular tastes, or one that an audience would (or could) quickly embrace. He easily recognized that this is an album which actually forces the desert island experience on a listener—whether the listener wanted to retreat to one or not.

He realized that *Trout Mask* was an endurance test for most listeners and it was a record that strongly divided and confounded more people perhaps than any other pop album. It may indeed be this very attribute that made *Trout Mask* such an inspired choice for a desert island disc, for it was conjured in that island's sequestered spirit long before the listener took the journey there. "One reason . . . that *Trout Mask Replica* would be my personal choice for a desert island is that a desert island is possibly the only place where I could play the record without being asked by friends and neighbors to take the damned thing off," Winner wrote. *Trout Mask Replica*, for Winner, provided a very succinct argument for desert island listening. "Created in isolation by a renegade artist/genius/madman and his band of unquestioning disciples, hermetic almost to the point of catatonia, yet challenging in every moment of its seventy-nine-minute duration, *Trout Mask* is a record uniquely suited to years and years of isolated listening," Winner further explained.

Trout Mask Replica earned its desert island exile because it has a way of spurning simple, or easy categorization. Throughout its twenty-eight tracks, the album mixes and combines various genres of music, including Delta blues, free jazz and expressionist lyricism, and does it at the speed of a Cuisinart. The record is a scrapbook collection of songs and poems, impishly acted out with Dadaist abandon and jack-in-the-box hijinks, performed with jagged rhythms and sharp conflicting atonal melodies. Ultimately, the record comes to raise important questions about just what constitutes musical entertainment and what an audience's relationship might be to it. "People like to hear music in tune because they hear it in tune all the time," Beefheart once told Robert Carey of the

New York Rocker. "I tried to break that all down on *Trout Mask Replica.* I made it all out of focus." It may be out of focus, but the music is never blurry.

According to Winner, Beefheart's most radical move was removing from his songs the security of harmony ("the mother's heartbeat," according to Beefheart), where we traditionally seek a warm spot in the songs we come to love. "Beefheart's music offers none of the qualities of a 'good' record; engaging melodies; a solid, interesting groove; poignant hook lines; and an intelligible reflection of the life of the listener," Winner explained. "If the purpose of a phonograph record is to soothe us, to provide a beat for dancing, a pulse for making love, a set of themes to reassure us in the joys and troubles of life's daily commerce, then *Trout Mask* fails utterly. . . . But if a record is legitimate in trying to overthrow our somnambulistic habits of hearing, seeing, and touching things, if it is valid in seeking to jolt our sensibilities and restructure the way we experience music and everything else, then Beefheart's strange collection of songs begins to make sense."

The songs themselves, though, are an odd lot in which to try and make sense. There may be no lulling melodies to draw us into the musical canvas of *Trout Mask*, but that doesn't mean that melodies don't exist. It's just that these spiky and jagged themes are quickly gone before we can catch them on first listen. The fleeting let's-try-it-on inventiveness of the compositions, in fact, comes across with a shocking ebullience. "It was a little like throwing a bomb," is how Tim Page, the former music critic at the *Washington Post*, described the initial impact of this album:

From the moment the phonograph needle settled into a Beefheart groove . . . everything changed. A crunching dissonance rent the air. Complicated time signatures and opaque poetry upset polite conversation and rattled the Mateus rose. Beefheart's roar of purest gravel and the untrammelled violence of the rhythms sent resident hippies into bummers; lovers could find no slow dances; young professors would sniff around the turntable, scrutinize the spinning disc, pronounce the music "Um . . . interesting," and then move as far away from the loudspeakers as possible. Meanwhile, a small but significant counterforce of Beefheart fans would surround the captured stereo, beaming with anarchic triumph.

Quoting composer Charles Wuorinen on Arnold Schoenberg's equally demanding *Pierrot Lunaire*, Page said that listening to *Trout Mask* is "rather like trying to befriend a porcupine." With "laughing-gas silliness aplenty," the album illustrated, for Page, the way Beefheart explored "the interface of two aesthetics that had never before been mated: namely, the heartfelt emotionalism of rhythm and blues and the cool celebration of high surrealism." That's a pretty good description of the bomb that Page claims had been hurled at listeners. But the record is also a mating of two other sources seldom acknowledged: the world of abstract expressionist painting and the urban blues ("Jackson Pollock trying to play like John Lee Hooker," is how Magic Band guitarist Bill Harkleroad accurately described the music to David Bowman of *Salon*).

Unlike many of the jazz artists and critics of the late 50s, rock fans (and rock critics) of the 60s and 70s seldom delved very far into the visual art world. "Music was always more accessible than art," said art critic Roberto Ohrt about rock audiences. "[The 70s] was a generation that regarded painting, in particular, as anachronistic, outworn, even decadent. Both concert goers and record collectors accepted and practised a degree of musical specialisation that outsiders often found positively grotesque, while any comparable degree of fanaticism applied to painting or to art in general was dismissed out of hand." Audiences may not have grasped just how much Beefheart (an abstract expressionist painter himself) drew upon that world in creating *Trout Mask Replica*. He treated music no differently than the way abstract expressionist painters, like Arshile Gorky or Jean Dubuffet, treated paint. Beefheart was after, in sound, the immediate sensation of musical color explosively hitting a canvas. The rock audience, largely unfamiliar with abstract art, couldn't truly account for the expressionism in Beefheart's record, since there was nothing in the pop music world to compare it to.

The sensibility at work in *Trout Mask* can also be tied to early twentieth century Dadaist sound poets like Hugo Ball, who mesmerized—and shocked—audiences in Zurich at the Cabaret Voltaire in 1916. "I shall be reading poems that are meant to dispense with conventional language, no less, and have done with it," Ball wrote in the *Dada Manifesto*. "I don't want words that other people have invented . . . I want my own stuff, my own rhythm, and vowels and consonants too, matching the rhythm and all my own. If this pulsation is seven yards long, I want words that are seven yards long." Like Ball, Beefheart chose to dispense with conventional language. He hypnotically tore into the syllables and consonants of his lyrics in quest of that pulsation. But unlike Ball, who was burdened by the solemn mysticism of Catholicism, Beefheart takes off—guilt-free—into the vapours by spinning yarns and springing puns. Just listen to a wildly playful song like "My Human Gets Me Blues" ("I knew you were under duress / I knew you were under yer dress"), where he subliminally channels poet Gregory Corso, who similarly got caught up in conceptual wordplay.

Although *Trout Mask Replica* is generally considered a landmark avant-garde rock record, it's essential to note that Beefheart and his group didn't set out to make an Art Statement—like the Dadaists. Declarations always have a clearly defined purpose, a political intent that fixes them in time. It makes for easy explanations and pigeonholing, too. For example, when Lou Reed made *Metal Machine Music* (1975), a two-record assault featuring nothing but sonic feedback, he clearly intended to outrage fans and annoy his record company. *Trout Mask* doesn't set out to deliberately anger anyone, even if it ultimately does, because Beefheart sincerely wants to entertain us. The record is also not in the adventurous cast of filmmaker Stan Brakhage, who decorated the film frame in *Mothlight* (1963) by pasting moth's wings onto film stock and then running it through an optical printer therefore making us aware of cinema's tactile qualities. Nor is Beefheart's record in the same world as Andy Warhol, when he extended the epic form of filmmaking in the somnambulistic *Empire* (1965), where we lay witness to a static shot of the Empire State Building for twenty-four-hours. Beefheart's effort is the exact opposite of minimalist art, it's as maximalist as music can get. Yet what ultimately makes *Trout Mask* a bigger artistic challenge than any of those other departures from convention is that, while it effortlessly tears apart the conventions of songwriting, it attempts it within the commercial world of pop. "I thought *Trout Mask Replica* was a very commercial album," Beefheart told Nick Kent of *New Musical Express* in 1974. "There was a lot of humour on that album that I thought people would pick up on." The lyrics, in particular, are written with such polymorphous glee and wit ("A squid eating dough in a polyethylene bag is fast 'n' bulbous. Got me?" is but one sample) that the record overturns any avant-garde solemnity. But the rock audience was still generally deaf to it. Defiantly original, *Trout Mask Replica* is a declaration of the American imagination that speaks in an unknown language, not fully comprehended, yet spoken candidly without fear of recrimination.

Within the lines of this story, at its very heart, is a bond between two men who were early best friends, artistic collaborators and later adversaries: Frank Zappa and Don Van Vliet. Many critics (including former Magic Band members) have attempted to diminish Zappa's role on this record. They suggest that he merely "slept at the switch," or simply pushed the record button. But those claims, specious as they are, seem to come out of a pathological dislike of Zappa and a romantic idealization of Beefheart as the hermit genius. Anyone who cares to truly listen to *Trout Mask* can feel the abiding spirit of both men on it. Those particularly familiar with Zappa's music, especially *Uncle Meat*, will hear the conceptual shape that Zappa, as a producer, gave to the production of the music on *Trout Mask Replica*. In terms of the creation of it, others elsewhere (particularly John French) have already illuminated the process by which the music was composed. Beefheart had for years (with the help of some critics) taken full credit for the record's songs, when it was actually created with the full involvement of the group. While many Beefheart fans might already be familiar with that part of the story, this book examines why Beefheart had the need to perpetuate that myth.

Most great albums do create myths around them and *Trout Mask Replica* is no different, but the reviews (both hostile and friendly) have usually overvalued and undervalued this great record in a deep need to find a critical language to understand it. Delving into the critical fallout of *Trout Mask Replica* is part of my own way, as a critic, of illuminating what the work means to me while leaving the judgements to the reader. Finally, the influence of this record goes further and deeper than I could have at first imagined. Besides the many groups who cite *Trout Mask* as a template for their own musical adventures, the songs on this record have been continually covered by numerous bands, while others have boldly taken their names from the song titles.

In the end, *Trout Mask Replica* is a full expression of one American artist's quest for total freedom. But it is also an expression of the tyranny of freedom. When you find yourself becoming the person you want to be, doing exactly what you want to do, sometimes freedom can't be sustained. For Beefheart, his earlier records designed an intricate map that tilted him toward *Trout Mask*, where he acquired the autonomy to remake rock and roll by breaking every rule in the genre. Yet even as the record caught his yearning for a new world, it was delivered with a foreboding force that stripped the ground out from under him. Whether the subsequent records were good or bad, Beefheart really had nowhere to turn after *Trout Mask Replica*. He could either refine the sound of it (*Lick My Decals Off, Baby*), define it for commercial consumption (*Clear Spot*), attempt to repeat it (*Bat Chain Puller*), or escape it (*Bluejeans and Moonbeams*). Once you find freedom, you often realize that you can never really keep it. "Men are freest when they are most unconscious of freedom," D.H. Lawrence once wrote of Americans. "The shout is a rattling of chains, always was." Beefheart's rattling of chains becomes the living drama of *Trout Mask Replica*. It's also the subject of this book. Beefheart's brand of freedom raised the very stakes of personal liberty for the man who envisioned it, the band who created it, and the audience who would soon discover it.

Chapter Two
A Different Fish

No author, without a trial, can conceive of the difficulty of writing a romance about a country where there is no shadow, no antiquity, no mystery, no picturesque and gloomy wrong, nor anything but a commonplace prosperity, in broad and simple daylight, as it is happily the case with my dear native land.

—Nathanial Hawthorne, *Transformation*

"If you want to be a different fish," Captain Beefheart once said, "jump out of school." The image of the fish, deeply rooted in Beefheart's art, had arrived long before the emergence of *Trout Mask Replica* in 1969. Yet rather than discovering it by jumping out of school, he first encountered it in one. Ten years before *Trout Mask* was conceived, Beefheart and his young buddy Frank Zappa stumbled upon a lone Webcor reel-to-reel tape recorder in an empty classroom at Antelope Valley Junior College in Lancaster, California. "[It] just happened to be sitting there waiting to be plundered—maroon, with the green blinking eye," Zappa recalled. One uneventful afternoon, in that vacant room, Beefheart, Zappa, and his brother Bobby improvised a parody of scatological blues called "Lost in a Whirlpool." It wasn't close to being their greatest collaboration, but the song celebrated in irreverent fashion their shared interest in the blues and R&B. You could hear a nascent affection in their performance of the kind usually found in shared juvenile camaraderie. The song came out of the foundation of a friendship, one that's formed when two outsiders suddenly find themselves killing time in an arid desert community. Looking back on the recording in 1993, Beefheart remarked, "Frank and I had a good time. We were just fooling around."

In 1972, though, the good times and the days of fooling around were clearly over. It had been three years since *Trout Mask Replica* had been released to rave reviews from critics like Lester Bangs who, writing in *Rolling Stone*, championed the record on release by calling it "the most unusual and challenging musical experience you'll have this year." BBC DJ John Peel, who helped launch a number of original bands from Half Man Half Biscuit to the Field Mice on his radio show, also contributed to the cheerleading, sending the record charging into the UK Top 50. "If there has been anything in the history of popular music which could be described as a work of art in a way that people who are involved in other areas of art would understand, then *Trout Mask* is probably that work," he proclaimed. The more adventurous critics and listeners brought glowing attention to the record, even if radio stations wouldn't dare touch it. None of that seemed to matter now to Captain Beefheart.

He suddenly had a huge axe to grind and he was looking for someone to help him sharpen it.

He began the year by discussing his career with Roy Carr, a journalist with the British music magazine *New Musical Express*. "I've had my fun," he said. "Now I'm going to make myself far more accessible to the public." Just what "accessible" might mean to the man who conceived *Trout Mask Replica* was never really explained. But it was clear that he didn't enjoy being perceived as a freak. The blame for that particular moniker was now laid at the door of *Trout Mask*'s producer, Frank Zappa. "Zappa is an oaf," Beefheart told Carr. "All he wanted to do was make me into a horrible freak. I am not a freak." Rejecting the tag of the freak was an odd denial considering that *Trout Mask Replica* represented the clearest representation of Captain Beefheart & the Magic Band's most radical work, setting them apart quite dramatically from most contemporary rock groups. Much of his chagrin, too, was directed toward the promotion of the record by Zappa's Straight Records. Beefheart was distressed about sharing space with such odd company as Wild Man Fischer, the GTO's, and especially Alice Cooper, who Beefheart thought killed live chickens as part of his stage act.

Beefheart was desperate to declare himself a true artist and not some circus act. "I am an artist . . . I paint, I write, I sculpt and I perform my own music," he pleaded. "The trouble with Frank Zappa is that he is not a good artist or a writer and by surrounding himself with good musicians and exploiting them, he boosts his own image." Beefheart provided for Carr his ultimate summation of the rancour between them: It's not worth getting into the bullshit to see what the bull ate. His disappointment was just as harsh when it came to describing his listening audience, whom he saw as "consisting of pickles." In other words, drug-addled zombies. "It hurts me," he said, "to see little girls sitting there looking like porcupines."

A few months later, he continued the tirade with Caroline Boucher of *Disc*, when he accused Zappa of "trying to keep the artist in me back." He went on to say that Zappa stole all his ideas in the early days, even using Beefheart's concepts for album titles (*Lumpy Gravy*, *Hot Rats*) without crediting him. "All this bit about being friends since we were young—I only met the guy about twenty-five times in the whole time I've been alive," he exclaimed. Suddenly the man who wished to be a different fish didn't want to be proclaimed as so different after all. It no longer mattered that he had finally found himself free to do the music he wished, on a record label and with a producer who offered it to him. It didn't help having at his disposal an amazingly skilled group of musicians dedicated to playing his music. Now he wasn't so satisfied with being different. "All the time, I have to explain myself to people," he told Boucher. "I actually have people trying to get me to explain why I have a right to be on this planet—hundreds of people a day." That right had suddenly become an ordeal, an albatross continuing to burden and enslave him. Freedom was defining him rather than the other way around. How did this happen—and so quickly—after the artistic success of *Trout Mask*? Perhaps it was much easier to be a free man when no one knew who you really were, when they didn't categorize you, or give a fuck about who you really were. To Captain Beefheart, that now seemed like eons ago.

Those days of yearning to be a free man existed before he met Zappa in 1956. Don Vliet, as he was known then, had attended Lancaster High School, where he possessed a passion for both drawing and sculpting. Earlier he had studied with Portuguese sculptor Augustonia Rodriguez and won a scholarship to study art in Europe. But his parents didn't approve the trip. For them, the art world was a haven for homosexuals all laying in wait to corrupt their only son. So when they moved to the Mohave Desert, they settled down in the safer white-bread community of Lancaster. They likely figured that, without much of an arts community, their son was safe there. But Don's folks couldn't anticipate his embracing of music. In particular, the work of other outsiders like blues giants Howlin' Wolf, Clarence "Gatemouth" Brown, and Sonny Boy Williamson. Vliet's growing fascination for the blues had been nurtured, in part, by the only musician in his family, his grandfather, Amos Warfield. Once a plantation owner in the South, Warfield was a white blues player who performed his songs using a lap guitar that he played with a pocketknife. It was through Amos that Don Vliet quickly acquired a natural fervour for that Delta sound. So when Vliet encountered Frank Zappa, he had found yet another outcast like himself, one who had a similar regard for blues and R&B.

On the day they met, Don was about to jump out of school, but not necessarily to be a different fish. His father, Glenn, who had a Helms bread truck route to Mohave, just suffered a heart attack and Don had to take over the job. Upon leaving school, Don just happened to give the spindly Zappa a ride home in his '49 blue powder Oldsmobile 88 Coupe. "[H]e was very fond of wearing khakis and French-toed shoes and dressing in the latest pachuco fashion," Zappa told British journalist Barry Miles. "It's a certain style of clothes that you had to wear to look like that type of teenager." Only it wasn't the dress of your average teenager—especially from Lancaster. However, Zappa was hardly your average teenager, either. At that time, he was becoming a local legend. He had not only formed the Blackouts, the only racially integrated R&B band in Lancaster, he had already begun experimenting with orchestral composition. Vic Mortensen, who was the drummer in Vliet's first group, the Omens, grew up in Claremont, California, where he first encountered Zappa. Appropriately enough, it was in the music room at their junior high school. Since Zappa began his musical life as an aspiring percussionist in the Blackouts, Mortensen was on hand to see him gathering all the school's drum sets and tuning them all to sound like tom-toms.

The Blackouts may have been a local phenomenon, but they didn't last, breaking up a year after Zappa met Don. At which point Zappa gave up the drums and started to turn his attention toward the guitar. More importantly, he was becoming seriously interested in becoming a composer. Besides his love of R&B, he had fallen in love with the avant-garde classical composer Edgard Varèse, who was challenging the very principles of western music, along with other serialist twelve-tone composers like Anton Webern and the neoclassicist Igor Stravinsky. When Vliet and Zappa encountered each other, Zappa was studying musical harmony while Vliet was still working on his art major. In short order, Don and Frank became fast friends over music and food. They'd gorge on Don's growing collection of rhythm and blues records, while also helping themselves to partially stale pineapple buns from Don's father's truck. "We'd start off at my house, and then we'd get something to eat and ride around in his old Oldsmobile looking for pussy—in Lancaster!" Zappa mused. When they couldn't get any local hot action, they'd be back at

Don's place eating buns and listening to records until 5AM. "It was the only thing that seemed to matter at the time," Zappa recalled wistfully. Music mattered quite a bit, to the point of zealous competitiveness. Often they would quiz each other on the records they listened to, testing each other's knowledge of an artist's work, the number of songs released, their B-sides, even the serial number on the single itself. It was at the height of this musical muscle-flexing that they happened on that magical Webcor reel-to-reel.

Zappa had been learning to play the guitar thanks to his brother Bobby's assistance. He was patterning his technique of playing on the sharp picking style of R&B artist Johnny "Guitar" Watson while adapting the aggressive tone of "Guitar" Slim. Don Vliet, on the other hand, was somewhat less assertive when it came to music. According to Beefheart biographer Mike Barnes, "[Vliet] would sing for his own amusement and obviously possessed talent, but he had to be cajoled or tricked into having his voice recorded." Barnes explained that Vliet would often become self-conscious and embarrassed when he performed, thus destroying his sense of timing. He would cover his awkwardness by becoming angry. When they gathered to record "Lost in a Whirlpool," Don had to be tricked into improvising the lyrics. "Without being kicked in the butt, he would never have started singing," Zappa explained.

For most of his career, Zappa's musical satire was largely based on his interest in documenting the unusual fixations of those normally not commemorated in pop songs—or for that matter, in classical music, too. For example, before his death, while working with the Ensemble Modern, he provided story material from *PFIQ* magazine—a magazine devoted to genital piercing—in order to create an orchestral composition. In "Lost in a Whirlpool," it was the peculiar story of a man being flushed down the toilet by his girlfriend where—to his horror —he encounters an eyeless brown fish. "There are few areas of basic human activity that have not been dealt with in rock 'n' roll, but a song about being pursued by a giant stool stands in a field of one," wrote Mike Barnes. But the idea of building a blues song around such questionable material was in keeping with a tradition much bigger than a field of one.

The blues has a long history embroidered with sexual slang and swagger—whether it was the Mississippi Sheiks' down and dirty "Ram Rod Blues" in 1930, Blind Boy Fuller's 1939 ode to cunnilingus, "I Want Some of Your Pie," or Hattie North's "Honey Dripper Blues." "Lost in a Whirlpool" plays havoc with that legacy by adding a touch of the preposterous. As the song opens, Bobby Zappa rhythmically starts strumming the melody, while brother Frank picks out the lead notes as if digging for gnats hiding in his guitar. Meanwhile, Don Vliet clears his throat. Once they establish the tune, Vliet bursts in with an uncharacteristic high falsetto reminiscent of Skip James in his 1931 "Cherry Ball Blues." "Weellll, I'm lost in a whirlpool," Vliet cries out in a mock despair, "Yeah, baby, my head is going round / Well, ever since my baby flushed me / Ohhh, been goin' round, yeah, round and round." As the singer swirls deeper and deeper into the commode, he quickly encounters the stool, that eyeless brown fish staring right back at him. Vliet momentarily slips back into his husky baritone, as if the shock from the rendezvous suddenly transforms him from this aggrieved lover into that of an outraged suitor. "He ain't got no eyes!" he stammers loudly before stating the obvious: "How could that motherfucker possibly see?" Vliet pleads for his lover to save him, perhaps with some Drano, or possibly a plunger, because, "I'm gettin' tired of all this pee." As the song concludes, Vliet lets loose with an improvised pun that, by the time of *Trout Mask Replica*, would be effortlessly supplied. "Don't go strangle Mother Goose," he warns. "Ooh, my head's in the noose." While the Zappa brothers continue to unfurl their endless chord progressions, Don decides to cap the tune with a quick "deedley-wee-wop." If "Lost in a Whirlpool" didn't produce anything astonishing, or terribly memorable, it did reveal something of the sensibilities of both men. You could clearly see the early origins of Zappa's penchant for bawdy humour, along with Vliet's style of inspired vamping. On that day, Frank Zappa officially began his quest to turn the history of popular music into a kaleidoscopic farce, while Don Van Vliet started to consider ways to transform the blues into an expressionist canvas for his own obsessions.

Since all his blues idols gave themselves names, often fierce ones chosen to live up to the force they would become in the world, Vliet wanted one himself. Chester Burnett had turned into Howlin' Wolf. McKinley Morganfield one day became Muddy Waters. But Don Van Vliet? He became Captain Beefheart. Vliet claims he coined it himself because he had "a beef in his heart" for the world. In truth, it was Frank Zappa who actually gave it to him, as part of a failed oratorio called *I Was a Teenage Maltshop*. This teenage "rock opera," which Zappa had called "a stupid piece of trash," was essentially a fantasy about a teenage Lone Ranger. In the film, there was to be a character called Captain Beefheart, featuring Vliet in the role. It was also the name of a character that Zappa created for another aborted film project called *Captain Beefheart vs.the Grunt People*.

As for the origin of the name Captain Beefheart, it was worthy of a Zappa song itself. Apparently Don's Uncle Alan (who Zappa claimed looked like Harry Truman) lived with his parents. "He used to piss with the [bathroom] door open when Don's girlfriend [Laurie] walked by, and [he'd] make comments about how his whizzer looked just like a beef heart," Zappa recalled. *Trout Mask* drummer John French concurred in substantiating that story. "There was an old joke about a fellow having 'a head on his penis the size of a beef heart,'" French explained. "From what I can surmise and from what I've seen of Frank, it seems likely that he combined a childhood hero image (à la Captain Midnight) with the old joke to come up with this distorted comic symbol for 'the kind of male sexuality.'" The name soon started to take on mythical status in the studio right after the day's recording. Vic Mortensen and Zappa would sit around devising clever band names and they'd start riffing on the character of Captain Beefheart. "[He] was supposed to be this magical character," Mortensen recalled. "His thing is [that] he would drink the Pepsi Cola and he could make magic things happen, he could appear or disappear." Mortensen suggested that if he had those kinds of powers, he should also have a band to match them. "I told Frank, 'Hey wouldn't it be cool if Captain Beefheart had a Magic Band, and wherever he went, if he wanted the band to appear, he would take a drink of Pepsi, and BINGO there's the band right behind him, 'jukin'?'"

In the summer of 1963, right after Zappa had bought his own five-track recording studio in Cucamonga named appropriately Studio Z, Don Van Vliet was born as Captain Beefheart. "Hello there kids, this is your old friend Captain

Beefheart," Vliet announced on tape in a carny barker's voice. "You know me—the Magic Man, invisible and all that jazz. Hah! I fly through time and space, dimension warp . . . all that rhythm. Well, anyway . . . I'm here tonight to tell you that we have a heck of a little teenage opera for ya. You're really gonna dig it . . . hmm . . . yes, it's really groovy." As groovy as it might have been, the grooves themselves never reached the ears of the public until years later when Zappa included excerpts on his commemorative *Mystery Disc* albums.

Before Captain Beefheart started playing pranks with his own Magic Band, he began singing in a new Zappa ensemble known as the Soots. Besides featuring Beefheart on vocals, the group included guitarist Alex St. Clair Snouffer and Vic Mortenson on drums. With the band, Don started gaining more and more confidence as a singer. They made a number of recordings including Little Richard's "Slippin' and Slidin'" (sung in the style of Howlin' Wolf) and "Metal Man Has Won His Wings," where Beefheart performed in the hallway outside the studio while the band played in the other room. This rather unorthodox technique for recording vocals was an early variation on the methods Zappa haphazardly developed for the sessions on *Trout Mask Replica*. Ultimately, Zappa sent their recordings for consideration to Dot Records, but Milt Rogers, the A&R guy at Dot, wrote him in December 1963 with some bad news. "[Although] the material has merit," Rogers stated, "we don't feel strongly enough about its commercial potential. . . ." Zappa phoned Rogers for a further explanation, and he was told that Dot's lack of interest was due to the "distorted guitar." On the positive side, he had nothing bad to say about Beefheart's voice.

While Zappa opened the door for Beefheart to ultimately

conceive *Trout Mask Replica*, Alex Snouffer provided a sufficient playhouse for him to ply his talents. Snouffer had been a student at Antelope in the late 50s, as well, and was a classmate of both Zappa and Beefheart. He also used to share in the record listening sessions at Vliet's house. Back when Zappa was wrestling gigs with the Blackouts, Snouffer was forming his own R&B band called the Omens. "[We] played early rhythm and blues during Little Richard's heyday and after that era," Snouffer explained. "Back then, it was Top 40 stuff." By the time Beefheart was performing with the Soots, Snouffer had left the Omens to do a paying gig at a Lake Tahoe casino. When he returned in 1964, he was itching to do some blues. "Don was one of the first people I went to see 'cause he and I had been pal-ling around together before I left," he recalled. Snouffer also sought out some other local musical pals: bassist Jerry Handley, who was a huge fan of John Lee Hooker and Jimmy Reed, plus guitarist Doug Moon, who had replaced Snouffer in the Omens when he'd set off to Tahoe. The idea was to form another blues band featuring Beefheart as their lead vocalist—even though he was hardly an experienced singer by that time. What sold Snouffer, though, was what he heard when Beefheart began to sing. "[H]e started to do this Howlin' Wolf imitation and I thought, 'Yo buddy!' This isn't bad at all," he explained. Besides, Beefheart had learned to play a mean blues harp. So Snouffer brought Moon and Handley into the group, while Beefheart nabbed Vic Mortensen for the drums. Captain Beefheart & the Magic Band began as imaginative fodder for Frank Zappa's failed film project, but now they were about to become a real live blues band.

Chapter Three
Jumping Out of School

Know to recognize and pick up the signs of the power we are awaiting, which are everywhere; in the fundamental language of cryptograms, engraved on crystals, on shells, on rails, in clouds, or in glass; inside snow, or light, or coal; on the hand, in the beams grouped round the magnetic poles, on wings.

Tristan Tzara, "Note on Poetry (1919),"
Seven Dada Manifestos and Lampisteries

For close to eighty minutes, *Trout Mask Replica* unleashes a cascade of atonal sounds that never relent. If the record itself provides both contrast and texture within that dissonance, the force and originality of those arrangements can leave you breathless, guessing as to how, even why, Captain Beefheart & the Magic Band arrived there. Usually, at the core of pop music is a quest for a sound which touches a nerve, something that strikes a pleasurable chord in the listener. The best pop tends to unify the incompatible world around it—even answer a subliminal calling. When Elvis cut loose in the 50s, he shook up a generation clearly ready to be shook—he uncorked a bottle filled with a frustrated generation's desire to stand apart from the herd. Elvis not only transcended what came before him, he validated everything good to come later.

In general, pop music is about the celebration and sharing of good times. For example, in the 60s, when the Ronettes sang "Be My Baby," you shared the intense joy in their voices. It was overwhelming to immerse yourself in such pleasure and still not lose yourself. You could melt into their sound and still be set apart from the herd. The Ronettes offered a kinship, a spiritual bond so rich, so generous, that they quenched a longing, a craving for something impenetrably beautiful to experience. Be my baby, NOW! they demanded—with a desire that made you feel a fool to resist it. Of course, the Beatles scaled those peaks continuously, too, even building greater expectations on the songs they left behind. On "Eight Days a Week," John Lennon easily convinced you that his love had the power to extend the calender beyond the expected seven days. He did it in a voice that asked—no, *demanded*—that those deeply expressed sentiments be shared and requited.

Yet long after the 60s, when (to invert John Sebastian's idyllic plea) no one believed in magic anymore, pop artists still reached for a sound that could bond with the listener and sum up an epoch. Long after the Beatles' hurricane of love subsided, and the punk storm blew over, Kurt Cobain of Nirvana created his own pop tempest out of the dissipation of an era. For Cobain, honest feeling was being replaced by vague cynicism and glib hipness. You could hear the recoil in his voice under the rage of the clanging guitars and Dave Grohl's cannon-shot drumbeat. His aside of "Oh well . . . whatever . . . nevermind" in their anthem, "Smells Like Teen Spirit" was the sound of defiance being bled dry in an emotional vacuum. Yet the urgency of the music ripped through the radio with the force of the Who. Cobain's voice was a drone of impacted rage, exploding only on the chorus. That explosion, though, brought listeners together as one. However, Cobain didn't stand in front of the song, as Elvis did in "Hound Dog," or the way Lennon could in "Eight Days a Week." He also didn't have the dynamism of Ronnie Spector in "Be My Baby." Cobain chased the song instead of riding it out. His was the exigency of emotional exhaustion, a man in dire straits to catch a runaway bus. "Smells Like Teen Spirit" collected the ennui of its time and blasted its contents with such vigour that it may be the most joyful song ever written about joylessness. Paradoxically, the song was often misunderstood as an expression of lethargic apathy, when it was actually a wince in the face of feelings that were too painful to consider. Nevertheless, whatever mood these varied pop songs (from Elvis to Nirvana) conveyed of their time, the largeness of their vision encompassed something already rumbling in the culture, if not already desired in the audience they reached out to. These artists built foundations for people to dream on.

By contrast, the tracks on *Trout Mask Replica* speak directly to no one and to nowhere. They're not only songs out of time, they don't even pretend to keep time. They catch you unaware because, unlike all those previous tunes, they're not tissue samples of their age. Their impact on the listener is fresh and shocking because they don't quench a thirst, they build an appetite. You may recognize familiar musical strains, but if you try to trace those strains, the record will tie you up in knots. It wasn't simply that the album's cryptic songs, recitations, and instrumentals were gumming you up; it was the actual clatter of the instruments and voices working together. These musicians weren't after a unified sound or a shared vision like all those other pop artists. These guys were testing the laws of gravity.

In the 60s, the decade in which *Trout Mask* erupted, there was mostly a joyful quest in the music. Every song— by seduction or force—seemed designed to harmonize all the disparate pieces of the culture. But Beefheart's Magic Band operated with an entirely different alchemy. The musicians pitched risky musical questions into the equation. "If I play my own rhythmic pattern, will it still connect to what the bass player, the drummer, and the singer are doing?" each one asked. The record became a search, not for the whole, but rather a definition of its individual parts. "*Trout Mask* sounds like the most democratic record ever made," Magic Band guitarist Bill Harkleroad remembers today. "All the instruments have an equal say in the overall plot." But it did more for Harkleroad than just define the role the instruments would play. "[It shaped] the way I think about music," he recalled. "I might like a bass player to stay more in the pocket than that, but having the bass to be as melodic as the melody instruments, rather than be simply a timekeeper, that is really striking to me." It was striking to listeners, as well, even if they didn't really know why.

Charlie Parker changed jazz soloing by playing within the chords of the piece rather than within the melody. Beefheart & the Magic Band, however, performed music that reduced the melody to the individual sounds of the instruments, as if each were a piece of sculpture. "The best description [of *Trout Mask*] that I can come up with is to call it sound sculptures," Harkleroad explained. "It was both polyphonic and polyrhythmic—with some repeated shapes. We would play in various time signatures, often at the same time. For instance, one part might be in 3/4 time while another was in 4/4 time. Only when they touched down together after twelve beats would we move on to the next section of the piece. . . . You'd hold on to your part for dear life against the thrust of what everybody else was doing."

Many years ago, jazz trumpeter Louis "Satchmo" Armstrong, the great traditionalist, attended a rehearsal of Dizzy Gillespie's group. Armstrong had once altered the art form of jazz by radically redefining the role of the soloist within the band. He was now the reluctant witness to the work of an inheritor. But this inheritor was a "be-bopper," changing all the rules of a music that Armstrong once revolutionized. After hearing a mere sample of this radical new sound from Gillespie's group, Armstrong quickly approached him. In a backhanded compliment from the past to the present, Satch told Dizzy, "You know, you have to know how to play pretty damn good before you can learn to play that bad." In the years leading up to *Trout Mask Replica*, Beefheart and his group became pretty damn good themselves—before they learned to play that bad.

* * *

They may have been billed as Captain Beefheart & the Magic Band, but it was definitely Alex Snouffer's group. For without Snouffer, it was doubtful that Don Van Vliet would have ever had opportunity—or even the desire—to be their lead singer. Vliet would later tell John French, "Alex was the dictator of the group—from his Prussian background—he came to me and told me, gave me an order, more or less, that I was going to sing in his band." For the first few months in 1964, the group would hold their practices at Jerry Handley's house where they would perform old blues songs and do Rolling Stones covers. Vic Mortensen would book their dates in the Lancaster area, while Snouffer would run the rehearsals, showing the individual musicians which parts to play and introducing them to their repertoire.

In April 1965, after performing a number of dances and Battle of the Bands contests, the group finally landed a show at the Teenage Fair, an annual rock event held at the Palladium in Hollywood. Besides taking them out of their usual desert digs, the gig provided a glimpse of their future. First of all, sixteen-year-old John French first encountered them at the show. "I was playing there in a surf band called the Maltesemen," French recalled. "Our first performance was in a booth, and next to our booth was a band that seemed very strange to me." The strange group he was encountering was an LA blues outfit called the Rising Sons. They featured a tall black singer named Taj Mahal, a bass player named Gary Marker, a bald drummer called Ed Cassidy (who would later join Spirit), and a brilliant slide guitarist known as Ry Cooder.

The great gospel singer Pop Staples had once said that Cooder's playing had a way of haunting him. "[Cooder sent] shivers down my spine," Staples explained. "[He] comes out with this old tune your parents taught you, and it [was] like going back in time." Cooder played the blues like some shapeshifting musical alchemist, a crafty archaeologist whose records took you places that were seemingly long hidden from the rest of the world. Eventually, he would become one of the finest session men in demand. A self-taught guitarist, Cooder began his musical life transfixed by the blues music of Josh White. White's version of the traditional folk ballad "House of the Rising Sun" had made a lasting impression on him, as it would also on Dave Van Ronk and Bob Dylan (who would later even steal Van Ronk's arrangement in order to record it on his first record).

Most of Cooder's teenage years were spent at an LA blues club called the Ash Grove. The club became his personal laboratory for experimentation, where he would learn the mandolin and the banjo, and play with a variety of people including singers Jackie De Shannon and Gary Davies. By 1964, he had already mastered the bottleneck blues guitar style that would, years later, become his stock in trade. It was during one of those occasions that Taj Mahal wandered into the Ash Grove in search of a kindred spirit and found one in Cooder. Before long, they formed the Rising Sons (in honor of Josh White) and began work on their first record. They would break up before that record would ever be finished, but not before their debut performance at the Teenage Fair. Their impact on Captain Beefheart & the Magic Band was about as indelible as Josh White's was on Cooder. It didn't go unnoticed by the

Rising Sons. "We were playing 'Travelling Riverside Blues,' and here's this weird guy [Beefheart] with long hair and big bright baby blue eyes, wearing a big leather coat," Sons' bass player Gary Marker recalled. "On one of the breaks, I see him lean over and grab Doug [Moon] by the arm and he gets this really angry look on his face. He points at Cooder and he says, 'There! That's the shit I'm talkin' about! That's what I want you to play!'" Moon stood there with a terrified look, according to Marker, wondering just how the hell he was going to sound like Ry Cooder—since, even at seventeen, Cooder sounded as seasoned as he does today. At that moment, Beefheart started considering ways to entice Cooder into the Magic Band.

Another fortuitous meeting took place after the show. A promoter named Dorothy Heard had taken interest in the band and told them that she could hook them up with agent Leonard Grant. With Grant at the helm, she felt, the band would start getting jobs at various colleges and auditoriums. She was right. He got them gigs in the Whisky-a-Go-Go in both Los Angeles and Denver. Grant also signed the group to a two-single deal at A&M Records in 1966. But just before they could start recording, Vic Mortensen got his draft notice for duty in Vietnam. With their drummer now AWOL, Snouffer decided to switch from guitar to drums. As a replacement, they hired a new guitarist, Rich Hepner, from a Denver band called the Jags. Their first recording session was scheduled for Sunset Sound Recorders on Sunset Boulevard in Los Angeles, where their producer was slated to be David Gates.

In retrospect, it may seem a deeply perverse joke that David Gates, later the vastly successful leader of the MOR soft-rock group Bread ("Baby, I'm a Want You"), would have anything to do with a group as idiosyncratic as Beefheart's. But, at that time, Gates was something of an adventurous producer, one eagerly seeking out distinct talent. He was also a great R&B fan with good taste. His favorite song just happened to be Bo Diddley's mid-50s hit "Diddy Wah Diddy," and he was dead right in figuring that it was a perfect tune for Beefheart to sing. He didn't have much choice, in any case, since the band didn't have much in the way of original material to record.

By 1966, Captain Beefheart & the Magic Band were playing the kind of electric blues music already having a huge revival in Britain. In the early part of the decade, white Brits such as Alexis Korner, John Mayall, the Rolling Stones, the Yardbirds, and, later, Peter Green's Fleetwood Mac and Cream built their careers doing cover tributes of their blues heroes. This included covering a vast catalogue of songs by Elmore James, Robert Johnson, John Lee Hooker, Slim Harpo, Muddy Waters, and Howlin' Wolf. While in America, the home of these icons, white blues bands took a different approach to the music. Perhaps being a little too embarrassed to earnestly try and imitate their betters, they mixed the blues together with a very basic, more rough-edged rock sound. While doing so, they kept the blues rhythm, which was perfect for AM radio airplay, but it also stripped the music of its soul. Many bands like the Amboy Dukes ("Baby, Please Don't Go"), Count Five ("Psychotic Reaction"), the Leaves ("Hey Joe"), Haunted ("125"), and the Standells ("Dirty Water"), found new life out of a blues hybrid that came to called "garage rock."

At the time they recorded "Diddy Wah Diddy,"

Beefheart's group superficially resembled a garage rock band, but Don's powerhouse voice and nimble harp playing gave them a blues authenticity. Once again, credit David Gates, who kept the blues spirit alive by giving this jabbing song a grungy veneer. "[Gates] came up with the idea of plugging the bass directly through the board so he could control it better," Jerry Handley explained. "I could see the glass in the booth shaking." Since it was rare to hear a bass cranked up so high in the mix, Handley loved hearing that glass rattle. But so did Vliet, whose voice and harp tore through the song. Snouffer recalled Gates, like a field general, pushing Beefheart beyond himself. "I mean, he was telling Don, 'I want high notes on the harp *here*,'" Snouffer remarked.

On first listen, "Diddy Wah Diddy" resembles "a freight train coming through your speakers," just as Handley would remember it. With the distorted fuzz tone of his bass pulling us into the song, Beefheart starts wailing on his harp with the speed and fury of Sonny Boy Williamson:

> I got a gal in Diddy Wah Diddy
> Ain't no town and it ain't no city
> She loves a man till it's a pity
> Crazy 'bout my gal in Diddy Wah Diddy.

He sings it with gusto and confidence. To augment the coarse blues/rock sound, Gates added a harpsichord on the bridge which gave the rough edges of the song a quaintly colourful palette. This powerful single debuted in April 1966, but it failed to chart—except in California, where DJ

Wolfman Jack heard a soulmate in the howl of Beefheart's voice. The commercial failure of the song, though, lay not so much with the track itself as it did with its timing. Apparently, an East Coast outfit from Boston called the Remains had simultaneously released "Diddy Wah Diddy" as their first single. That version dominated radio airplay in the east, while Beefheart won the West Coast.

David Gates oversaw a number of Beefheart songs at the A&M sessions including the punchy "Frying Pan," "Here I Am, I Always Am," and "Who Do You Think You're Fooling?" But he also decided to contribute a pop song himself called "Moonchild," a tune he thought was "pretty out there." Others, however, thought it was pretty out to lunch. While trying for an elliptically poetic effect ("Every time there's a full moon up above / Then she's out of this world"), Gates fashioned the kind of pop oddity that made Beefheart sound more like a spiritual cousin to Rod McKuen. "Well, let's put it this way, ['Moonchild'] was never our 'cup of tea,'" Snouffer said diplomatically. Nevertheless, Gates decided to release it as their next single backed with the much superior "Frying Pan." Not only did it flop, it created a huge dissension within the band. The argument led to the departure of Leonard Grant and guitarist Richard Hepner, forcing Alex Snouffer off the drum kit and back on guitar. But the failure of "Moonchild" did have one positive effect: Beefheart started writing more and more original material.

One of those new songs was an innovative psychedelic blues track called "Electricity"—and it placed the final nail in the group's coffin at A&M Records. With the lyrics co-written by Herb Bermann, a poet/playwright Vliet had recently met, "Electricity" diverted dramatically from the basic blues of "Diddy Wah Diddy." When co-founder Jerry Moss heard lyrics like "Midnight cowboy stains in black reads dark roads without a map / To free-seeking electricity," he lost his bearings. He immediately described the tune as "too negative" for the label—even deeming it too dangerous for his daughter's mental health. A&M decided to drop the group from their roster. Since there was no immediate interest in the pure voltage of Beefheart's revamped poetic output, the band withdrew to lay the foundations of what would unwittingly evolve into *Trout Mask Replica*.

* * *

When the band retreated to Beefheart's mother's house in the fall of 1966, with no recording contract, they were in disarray. Yet Vliet seemed to thrive on the chaos within the group. For one thing, he began composing more songs that broke from the traditional blues and R&B forms. He began providing some new direction as well by slowly taking over the band from Snouffer. Since Beefheart wasn't technically gifted, he initially conveyed his ideas by translating them through Doug Moon. "I would fall into a little riff maybe that I heard off a blues album, and Don would pick up on something: 'Hey! Keep doing that, Man!'" Moon recalled. Vliet would then grab lyrics, written on scraps of paper, from a brown paper bag and compose songs based on Moon's chord changes—just as he would a few years later on the acoustic blues track "China Pig" from *Trout Mask Replica*. He would devise a musical shorthand by whistling and humming melodies, as Thelonious Monk often did with his ensembles, to teach the band the new songs. But he was becoming more and more obsessed with including Ry Cooder and finding ways to get rid of Doug Moon.

Beefheart began his little coup by bringing some new blood into the band. He called up John French and invited him to join. "Don called and said, 'This is Don Vliet, do you know who this is?' French remarked. "Then very hesitantly: 'Do you wanna, ah—well, I was wondering if you'd like, ah—I was thinking—maybe you would like to blow drums with us?'" Vliet looked up Gary Marker from the Rising Sons, with whom he had now developed a stronger friendship after the Teenage Fair gig. It was Marker, a former jazz player, who introduced him to the modern jazz of Ornette Coleman and Roland Kirk. Besides inspiring Beefheart's own interest in the saxophone, the exposure to modern jazz helped influence many of the conceptual ideas found on *Trout Mask*.

What began to distinguish the new songs from the old, though, was the increasing presence of marijuana and hallucinogens, which were introduced into the mix by Beefheart's cousin Victor Hayden, a long-haired urchin, who would later be dubbed the Mascara Snake on *Trout Mask Replica*. Since grass is a very social drug, it encouraged the group to work together, even if their rehearsals resembled an ad hoc pot party. The material naturally started to grow more strangely abstract and complex, with psychedelic overtones. "Autumn's Child," for example, also co-written with Herb Bermann, was an early blueprint for many of the songs on *Trout Mask Replica*. Once again invoking the image of the fish out of school seeking personal freedom, Beefheart sings:

> Harvest moon be nimble
> Apples bob and tremble
> Fish pond streaks love kind
> Found the child I had to find.

Other unusual items emerged, like "Plastic Factory," which Don co-wrote with Jerry Handley and which evoked the ecological concerns later found on *Trout Mask*'s "Ant Man Bee":

> Bee 'n flower growin'
> Boy 'n girl are glowin'
> Fac'trys no place for me
> Boss man let me be.

Other R&B-flavoured tracks like "Call on Me" and "I'm Glad" were being considered for the group's first record—whenever they could find an interested label. Soon all of this would be remedied.

After many band meetings, Beefheart insisted that the group move to LA once they were dropped by A&M. There was good reason for the maneuver. The Magic Band had drawn interest from Bob Krasnow, the California head of Kama Sutra Records. Krasnow had been a huge fan of "Diddy Wah Diddy" and was hoping to sign Beefheart to Kama Sutra's new subsidiary, Buddha Records. But not all the band members saw light at the end of this tunnel. "A lot of problems started to surface then," Doug Moon remembered. "People were doing drugs and one thing or another. When we left Lancaster we got into the influence of LA—all the people and stuff down there—and it got crazy. Don was listening to everybody. And everybody had their own opinion. The band, at some point in there, lost its soul." Whether the group was losing its soul was up for debate, but they were certainly about to lose Moon, who was being singled out for "incompetence" by the Captain. Although Moon was a perfectly competent player, Beefheart was desperate to squeeze Cooder into the group. When it became clear to Gary Marker that Moon was being prepped for departure, he sought out his old bandmate. Marker convinced Cooder that, even though in name it was Captain Beefheart & his Magic Band, it could easily be the Ry Cooder Group.

It turned out that Krasnow was just as eager as Beefheart to have Cooder in the Magic Band. He even called up Cooder and told him that Captain Beefheart & the Magic Band were "going to be the biggest thing since the Beatles, bigger than the Beatles." The hyperbole was definitely enticing to Cooder, but it didn't alleviate his uneasiness. Cooder had already witnessed Doug Moon's emotional exhaustion from all the abuse he was taking from Don Van Vliet. After figuring that he shared many similar musical ideas with Beefheart, though, he relented anyway and joined the group. On Cooder's first day at rehearsals, he saw Moon's firing firsthand. "[Van Vliet said,] 'Well, I'll tell you what we're doing and what we're not doing," Cooder recalled. Pointing at Moon, Beefheart continued his tirade. "'Get outta here, Doug, just get outta here. You're no use to us now.'" To paraphrase Beefheart biographer Mike Barnes, the hornet's nest was being stirred.

* * *

When Doug Moon complained that the group was losing its soul, what he was perhaps perceiving was the dissolution of the band as a collaborative entity. Beefheart's quest to find democratic freedom in his art found him becoming something of an authoritarian to do it. The path to *Trout Mask Replica* was not outlined by the quixotic zeal of a group breaking all the rules to find themselves. It was etched by one man's narrow will to achieve his own artistic liberation. Within that ambiguous quest, casualties were certain. Since Alex Snouffer's guitar playing had waned during his stint as the group's drummer, Don Van Vliet was able to gain complete control of the band when Ry Cooder came onboard. Doug Moon's firing would turn out to be moot anyway. He didn't see any place for himself on the band's first record, *Safe as Milk*. "By the time the album finally came out, those songs had evolved to become a little bit more avant-garde and a little bit more hinting at things to come in Don's later albums," Moon explained to Elaine Shepherd of the BBC in 1995. "That was the transitional period and that's why I left, because of those influences. I did not have that calling. When it got a little too far out, a little too weird, unsyncopated and bizarre and avant-garde, it just did not work with me."

When *Safe as Milk* was released in September 1967, it was clear to anyone who heard it that Beefheart's music had begun to evolve dramatically from the basic blues style in which it began. They started doing the new record in

Sunset Sound, an eight-track studio, with Gary Marker engineering and Richard Perry, who would later produce a bevy of artists including Ringo Starr, Barbara Streisand, Harry Nilsson, and Burton Cummings, at the helm. Since Perry felt more comfortable working in a four-track setup, they moved to RCA Studios. Unfortunately, the change affected the overall sound of the album, which Jerry Handling especially thought made it less forceful than their single, "Diddy Wah Diddy." What it lacked in force, however, it made up in pure texture.

Out of the quiet, Ry Cooder's slide calls out to Beefheart, who answers in the opening blues tune, "Sure 'Nuff 'N Yes I Do." Based on Muddy Waters' "Rollin' & Tumblin'," Beefheart's lyrics for "Sure 'Nuff" point toward a more obscure American landscape than the Waters original. "I was born in the desert," Beefheart moans over the whine of Cooder's slide, "came up from New Orleans." After fusing his own birthplace with that of jazz and blues, Beefheart quickly reaches for the ethereal. "Came upon a tornado, saw light in the sky," he sings. "I went around all day with the moon stickin' in my eye." From there, the song gallops into an aggressive prowl filled with sexual adventure. "Got the time to teach ya now," Beefheart snears. "Bet you'll learn some too." From there, the record broadens its scope from the psychedelia of "Zig Zag Wanderer," the R&B doo-wop of "Call on Me," to the light pop of "Yellow Brick Road." In a sense, the record is a map of Beefheart's intent to transform varied blues and R&B forms, just as Frank Zappa's debut, *Freak Out!* did a year earlier.

While "Sure 'Nuff 'N Yes I Do" has the snake moan

sound of Beefheart's early material, there was nothing quite like the theremin-driven psychedelic blues of "Electricity." The theremin was the world's first electronic instrument, a precursor to the moog synthesizer, created by the Russian emigré Leon Theremin shortly after the turn of the twentieth century. It is the only electronic instrument that is played without ever being physically touched. The pitches are played electronically by slowly moving your hand over the base of the instrument. In the 20s and 30s, Theremin had launched an orchestra of theremin players performing a wide repertoire of nineteenth-century romantic music. But after he was mysteriously kidnapped by Russian government officials and disappeared, the theremin fell into the hands of avant-garde musicians and film composers who heard a more sinister world lurking in its unearthly wailing. Composer Miklos Rozsa, for instance, would use the theremin to indicate Gregory Peck's repressed fears in Alfred Hitchcock's *Spellbound* (1945). Rozsa would repeat the exercise using the theremin to depict Ray Milland's alcoholic delusions in *The Lost Weekend* (1945). In the 1951 science-fiction classic, *The Day the Earth Stood Still*, Bernard Herrmann would impart an otherworldly atmosphere by using it to provide ominous color to Klaatu's robot, Gort. Brian Wilson, in the Beach Boys' 1966 single "Good Vibrations," briefly returned the theremin to its more romantic origins, until Beefheart brought it back to the realm of spooky foreboding.

The theremin became part of "Electricity" actually by chance. Beefheart originally wanted Gary Marker to use the sound of a circular saw to create the buzz under his phrasing of EEE-LECC-TRI-CITTYYY, but it didn't mix too well. "His instincts were right but the technology wasn't there at the time," Marker explained. The theremin was used to duplicate the buzzing sound. There was nothing to duplicate the power of Beefheart's voice, though, when he blew out a $1,200 Telefunken microphone during the recording of his vocals. As for the syncopated drum part in "Electricity," Beefheart sang the rhythm guitar parts for John French to translate into the percussion section. This was a move that anticipated the style of arranging both men used on *Trout Mask*. If the white soul balladry of "Call on Me" was Beefheart at his most seductive, the Indian-influenced rhythms of "Abba Zaba" had him at his most transfixing—even if the song's subject matter concerned nothing more exotic than a peanut bar that features a baboon logo on the wrapper. According to Alex Snouffer, the guitar melody was lifted from a sitar lick heard on one of Ravi Shankar's album.

Despite the broad musical scope of *Safe as Milk*, the sessions were hardly seamless. While Alex Snouffer, Ry Cooder, Jerry Handley, and John French were well rehearsed, seasoned musicians, Beefheart was scattered as if he were perpetually caught in a windstorm. The windstorm, though, was of his own making, brought on by his trips on LSD which, according to French, led to acute hypochondria. "What followed were constant requests from Don to 'feel my heart' and 'check my pulse,'" French explained. "[I]t became a tedious, wearing, and stressful daily routine for the entire band." French had to organize Beefheart's lyrics, which he still kept on scrap pieces of paper. "[A]s I would work on one song, I'd put them in order on the floor and then write them down by looking at the scraps on the floor," he recalled. Since French didn't possess a typewriter, he'd print them out by hand. Richard Perry would then suggest to Beefheart where in the song each lyric would be sung.

Although the mixing of *Safe as Milk* became a long, laborious process, it resulted in a pop album that was filled with quick bursts of chimerical inspiration. Unlike many of the contemporary psychedelic records, ones that conceded to the trends of the moment, *Safe as Milk* challenged all others to keep up. Buddha Records, in particular, was hoping they could get some mileage out of Beefheart's success by having the group play the Monterey Pop Festival that summer in 1967. It's fascinating to consider just how Beefheart's band would have fit into a lineup that included the Byrds, the Mamas and Papas, Ravi Shankar, Janis Joplin, Otis Redding, the Who, and the landmark performance by Jimi Hendrix. However, a gig at a "Love-In" at Mt. Tamalpais in San Francisco changed all of that. Dressed in the natty suits of gangsters, rather than the rustic garb of hippies, they mounted a stage in a show they shared with Tim Buckley, Jefferson Airplane, and the Byrds. But Beefheart was on edge to begin with, feeling the anxiety of performing in front of a large audience, as well as tripping from heavy LSD usage. They started to play "Electricity," the second song in their set, when Beefheart stopped in middle of the song. "He just froze, turned, and walked off the back of the ten-foot stage, falling on top of [Bob] Krasnow," John French recalled. Once again, lost in a whirlpool, the omnipresent image of the fish reemerged to cause both panic and dread. Vliet had looked down at a girl in the audience during the song and watched as she turned into a vertebrate with gills and bubbles coming out of her mouth. Beefheart's reaction was to walk right off the stage with the hope that just maybe she'd catch him. She didn't—and the show ended.

Immediately after the performance, Ry Cooder decided to walk right out of the band. French tried to persuade him to stay until after the Monterey gig, but Cooder was exasperated by all the nonsense, not to mention the anxiety generated within the group by Don Van Vliet. "He's a Nazi," Cooder remarked. "It makes you feel like Anne Frank to be around him." Thanks to Beefheart's meltdown, the Monterey Pop Festival was not only definitely out, they had to scramble to find a new replacement for Cooder. Beefheart ultimately chose Jeff Cotton to be their new lead guitarist, alongside Snouffer, in October 1967. Cotton was basically a blues player who had once played with John French in Blues in a Bottle. He was an experimentalist eager to try new approaches to the genre. Cotton quickly moved into the band's digs in Laurel Canyon to begin work on what was to be the group's biggest gamble.

It Comes to You in a Plain Brown Wrapper was conceived as a complete reimagining of the American blues to be spread out over two records. With Bob Krasnow at the production desk, the group began recording sessions in TTG studios in Hollywood. On this record, Beefheart wanted to present a boldly new improvisational music integrating the Delta blues sound with the improvisational textures of modern jazz. The first recordings began as a series of long blues jams, slowly building songs like the astonishingly extemporized nineteen-minute epic "Tarotplane," where the group dipped into Robert Johnson's "Terraplane

Blues," caught echoes of Blind Willie Johnson's passionate plea "You're Going to Need Somebody on Your Bond," then added a sampling of Willie Dixon's saucy "Wang Dang Doodle" for good measure. Beefheart would call out verse after verse, punctuating each one with his squeaking blues harp. What Beefheart sought—and would actually find two years later on *Trout Mask*—was a music that was, as Greil Marcus once described, "as far ahead of its time as it was behind it." Beefheart was out to destroy what Frank Zappa would later call the affliction of time. In particular, how time imposes certain values on life and art, where innovative deviations from the norm get considered out of time, or ahead of their time—rather than timeless. "A lot of people think they have time, you see, and they put on a little circle on their wrists, which is really amusing: *keeping* time," Beefheart told *Downbeat* in 1971. Beefheart's long musical excursions were attempts to shatter time, make it irrelevant as a point of definition or reference, and rather explore it as an infinite playground with no imposed boundaries.

On "25th Century Quaker," Beefheart opens the song by introducing the shinei, an Indian reed instrument given to him by Ornette Coleman. He bends time along with the musical grain by wedding a flower child of the 60s, who has eyes "that flutter like a wide-open shutter," with a Quaker of the future. On "Trust Us," his answer to "We Love You," the Rolling Stones' 1967 drug bust anthem to their supportive fans, Beefheart calls out to trust us "before you turn to dust," stating that mortality is merely a dot that punctuates time. The abstract ballad, "Beatle Bones 'N' Smokin' Stones," is his reply to the Beatles' "Strawberry Fields Forever." John Lennon's beautifully mournful dirge about childhood lost, where time itself slipped away and became locked eternally into the caste of a Salvation Army orphanage. Beefheart's reply is an elliptical meditation on timeless bereavement. "Blue veins through grey felt tomorrows," Beefheart laments, "celluloid sailboat your own feathered kind, blow it into a pond swaying in circles."

Never losing sight of the blues, however, Beefheart castigated pretenders to the cause in "Gimme Dat Harp Boy." He invented dense blues figures for simple confections like "Kandy Korn." But it was "Mirror Man" that would become the skeleton key which opened the Pandora's box leading to *Trout Mask Replica*. Based on a 1966 piece performed in Lancaster by the now outcast Doug Moon, "Mirror Man" was an epic exploration, not only of the musical language of the blues, but of language itself. Beefheart breaks apart the phrases of the title into syllables and consonants. He invents puns on the spot ("Mirror Man is but a mere man") and transforms the song into sound fragments boldly illustrating a painter's love of splashing color on the canvas. "Mirror Man" wasn't an exercise in endless noodling, though, as was the fashion of the time by bands like Iron Butterfly ("In-A-Gadda-Da-Vida"). Beefheart was reshaping the power of the blues by altering the timbre of the music rather than its message. It became clear, while listening to "Mirror Man," that as the music became less formally structured, Beefheart was becoming more lyrically expressionistic. The group started to weave its way illustriously through the soundscapes emerging spontaneously out of these improvisations. "The guitars are not so much underpinned as jostled by French, whose drumming was becoming more individual—incisive accents incorporated into rolling, roaming tom-tom, snare, and hi-hat patterns," observed Mike Barnes.

After recording these tracks, Bob Krasnow sent the band on tour in Europe. It was hardly the second coming of Beatlemania. The first stop was in Germany, at a record convention, where they flopped due to poor sound brought on by lousy equipment. In London, because of a lack of work permits, they spent a night in a detention hall before finally playing on John Peel's BBC sessions. From there, it was Cannes, France, where they attended the MIDEM Music Festival, met Paul McCartney (who was there to receive an award), and played a set on the beach to some bewildered industry folks who safely kept their distance. When the band got home, there was still no release date on the new album. But should anyone be surprised that the label who put out the 1910 Fruitgum Co.'s "Chewy, Chewy" would respond so unfavorably to songs like "Tarotplane" and "Beatle Bones 'N' Smokin' Stones?" Krasnow assured them he'd work it out. He did so by disingenuously misfiling their Buddha contract so that the option wouldn't be picked up and he could sign them to another label. That label, Blue Thumb Records, an offshoot of Kama Sutra, was one that Krasnow created himself. Krasnow used the move to Blue Thumb to bankroll the recording sessions that would ultimately become *Strictly Personal*. (The material intended for the abandoned *Brown Wrapper* record would later in 1971 be released as *Mirror Man*.)

The *Strictly Personal* sessions got underway over eight days between April and May 1968. Some of the material intended for *Wrapper* found its way onto *Strictly Personal*, such as "Beatle Bones 'N' Smokin' Stones," "Trust Us," and "Safe as Milk." The new songs further developed the inventive blues model the group was already experimenting with. They recast Son House's "Death Letter Blues," a passionate song of grief over receiving a correspondence about a girl's passing, into "Ah Feel Like Ahcid." In the song, a surreal blues holler, the singer licks the LSD from a stamp and hallucinates her return as a duck/chicken "flapping" merrily down his street. The track was eventually cut into pieces and used as a leitmotif threading its way throughout the finished album. "Son of Mirror Man—Mere Man" became a more distilled version of "Mirror Man."

With the recording finished, the band hit the road. While on tour, however, Krasnow (in a state of stoned bliss on acid) secretly took the master tapes for *Strictly Personal* and littered them with various electronic phasing effects plus other psychedelic clamour to make the album more trendy and saleable—without getting permission from the group. In London, the band received a visit from Krasnow, eager to play them their newly remixed opus, as if he were Santa Claus coming to town. On first listen, John French was quite taken with all the murky compression used on the tracks. "We sat there in London, listening to it on this big sound system, and I kind of liked the way it sounded," French said excitingly. "I thought, well it's *contemporary*. It'll work for now." For Beefheart, on the other hand, it didn't work at all. He was so outraged that he immediately disowned it, even telling French that the effects sounded like "psychedelic bromo seltzer."

By June 1968, the tour was immediately aborted and the band was again in disarray. Although *Strictly Personal* arrived in stores by the fall, the musicians were starting to fall out. Some of them didn't care for the new direction the music was taking—despite the bromo seltzer. For one, Snouffer found the compositions too disorganized, as did Jerry Handling. They resented Beefheart's iron will and chaotic habits, as well. They saw no part for them in this evolving music, just as Doug Moon had earlier. But Don Aldridge, a friend of Beefheart's dating back to their days in Lancaster, saw other reasons for their departure—as well as the Magic Band's emerging musical mosaic. "I always will believe Frank [Zappa] was the catalyst," Aldridge told Mike Barnes. "Frank was actually becoming wealthy and famous doing what they had experimented with as kids. Don could not accomplish his goal with the *Safe as Milk* band."

It was true. By 1968, Zappa had accomplished a fair bit compared to Beefheart. When he abandoned Studio Z in Cucamonga in early 1964, Zappa had just been asked to join a local R&B bar band called the Soul Giants. The call came from their lead singer Ray Collins, who Zappa had played with earlier at Studio Z. They recorded a variety of surf rock and novelty comedy singles, including an affectionate doo-wop tribute for Cleave Duncan and the Penguins called "Memories of El Monte." While initially sticking to standard R&B fodder in their bar gigs, Zappa decided that if the group was going to go anywhere they should try doing original material—meaning, his own. He saw the group potentially as the antithesis of the cute pop bands now filling the charts. On Mother's Day 1964, with an image designed to scare your mother, they became the Mothers of Invention. (Because the simple phrase "the

Mothers" was street slang for a collection of motherfuckers, they had to—out of necessity—become the Mothers of Invention.) The repertoire Zappa provided for the group was a hybrid of the serialist classical school, R&B, doo-wop, and the blues, sprinkled with an abundance of social satire and irreverence. "I composed a composite, gap-filling product that fills most of the gaps between so-called serious music and so-called popular music," he would later write, describing it as his Project/Object.

The timing for Zappa's Project/Object was fortuitous because it began in the wake of a budding nonconformist freak scene in Los Angeles. The British Invasion had just sent American record companies on a mad search to find —and sign—any band that could write songs and play their own instruments. In LA, there was a huge folk music scene already beginning and merging with the rock being played in the clubs. One such club owner was Herb Cohen, a feisty political and musical activist, who was a promoter of folk artists like Odetta, plus blues performers Sonny Terry & Brownie McGhee. Cohen met Zappa during the filming of a faux tabloid documentary called *Mondo Hollywood*, which was supposed to reveal the shocking underside of the Hollywood freak scene. Although he didn't have a clue as to what Zappa's Project/Object was about, he did recognize both his talent and intelligence. He immediately became the band's manager.

By July 1966, the Mothers of Invention had secured a contract at MGM/Verve Records, the prestigious jazz label. They'd also landed producer Tom Wilson, who had produced landmark jazz records in the 50s by avant-garde pianist Cecil Taylor (*Jazz Advance*) and saxophonist John

Coltrane (*Coltrane Time*), as well as working the controls for Bob Dylan's "Like a Rolling Stone" in 1965. Their debut, *Freak Out!* was a double-LP concept album that provided a provocative, eclectic chart of Zappa's Project/Object—drawing on all his influences from Varèse to Richard Berry ("Louie Louie"). The record was a cornucopia of American musical genres, including doo-wop parodies ("Go Cry on Somebody Else's Shoulder"), sophisticated R&B arrangements ("How Could I Be Such a Fool?"), abstract dissonant rock ("Who Are the Brain Police?"), an outlandish tribute to both Igor Stravinsky's ballet scores and the Igor of horror movies ("The Return of the Son of Monster Magnet"), social protest blues ("Trouble Every Day"), and political advocacy ("Hungry Freaks, Daddy").

In 1967, the Mothers' second album, *Absolutely Free*, was an absurdist oratorio. "We play the new free music—music as absolutely free, unencumbered by American cultural suppression," Zappa explained. To pull it off, Zappa hired some highly gifted sight-reading musicians—Bunk Gardner on saxophone and Don Preston on keyboards—to augment the bar band veterans. The idea was to create an ensemble that dissolved the imposed boundaries between the "low culture" of rock and roll and the "high culture" of orchestral music. Zappa would follow up *Absolutely Free* with a solo orchestral album, *Lumpy Gravy*, a ballet score that resembled a cross between a *Mad* magazine collage and Karlheinz Stockhausen. The orchestral music, played by an ad hoc session group called the Abnuceals Emuukha Electric Symphony Orchestra, was continually broken up by snatches of random dialogue, *musique-concrète*, surf rock, and cartoon tone clusters suggesting a radio dial madly spinning across the network.

Later in the year, the Mothers would reconvene to skewer the hippie utopianism of the previous Summer of Love on *We're Only in it for the Money*, which used the Beatles' sunny *Sgt. Pepper's Lonely Hearts Club Band* as their point of parody; create a neo-classical appraisal of 50s doo-wop on *Cruising with Ruben & the Jets*, and begin *Uncle Meat*, the fullest design of the Project/Object. It was perhaps this particular record that would have a significant impact on Zappa's production of *Trout Mask Replica*. Originally to be a soundtrack for the Mothers' first film (which was incomplete due to lack of financing), *Uncle Meat* became a surreal scrapbook of personal and musical history. To play the difficult and complex scores, Zappa first added more highly experienced players such as Ruth Komonoff on marimba and Ruth's future husband, Ian Underwood, on a variety of wind and keyboard instruments. The record combined clips of the band cutting loose ("King Kong"), audio-verité of band members complaining about poverty ("If we'd all been living in California"), performances of tricky electronic serialist scores ("Zolar Czakl," "We Can Shoot You"), brilliantly dense cross-pollinations of doo-wop and serialism ("Dog Breath, in the Year of the Plague"), and ample samples of their stage absurdities like "Louie Louie" being played on the pipe organ at the Royal Albert Hall in London. In 1968, when Beefheart encountered him, Zappa was preparing an album that was essentially an anthropological musical study of the Mothers of Invention. It would not only serve as a documentary collage of the band's progress; *Uncle Meat* would document and define their place in the lexicon of American popular music.

Although Zappa was making huge progress as a composer, by the time of *Uncle Meat*, he was (like Beefheart) having contractual difficulties with his label. But unlike Don Van Vliet, Zappa was a businessman who thought of his work in terms of business. In December 1967, he discovered that Verve had made the mistake of not picking up the option on his contract with the label. So Zappa and Herb Cohen decided to use that as leverage to negotiate a deal to create a logo within the company. It was to be called—appropriately enough—Bizarre Productions. Their logo was a nineteenth-century picturesque engraving of a vacuum pump. Initially, Mothers' albums on Bizarre would be released through MGM/Verve, until 1969, when Warner Brothers would acquire the production label. Zappa and Cohen formed Bizarre/Straight Records for Herb Cohen's most unconventional artists. "We make records that are a little different," Zappa made clear in his mission statement. "We present musical and sociological material which the important record companies would probably not allow you to hear." He then added with caustic irony: "Just what the world needs . . . another record company."

We're Only in It for the Money, released in January 1968, became the first album under the Bizarre logo. However, the first record showcasing one of Bizarre's unusual finds appeared that summer. It was called *An Evening with Wild Man Fischer* and you certainly couldn't accuse it of being in it for the money—or predicting it ever to make any either. *An Evening with Wild Man Fischer* was a collection of a cappella folk songs by an aggressive and alarming busker named Larry "Wild Man" Fischer. Fischer was born in

Los Angeles in 1945, and he became a familiar figure along the Sunset Strip in the mid-60s. While making his living spontaneously composing his own songs for small change, he'd actually been institutionalized by his mother after attempting to kill her. Fischer was homeless and jobless, hanging out at clubs along the Sunset Strip. The subsequent double album, produced by Zappa, gathered his street recordings and monologues in the studio, as well as songs featuring percussion overdubs. The unsettling montage cover was by Cal Schenkel, Zappa's in-house cover artist, and it featured the deranged Fischer holding a knife to the throat of a cardboard cut-out woman (who many assumed to be his mother).

An Evening with Wild Man Fischer demonstrated Zappa's specialized interest in music as a sociological construct. Each individual he signed to his new label had a distinctive mould he wished to uncork. "There's some people that break that mould and in that moment they're who they really are, and Frank could always pull that out of somebody," his wife Gail Zappa explained. "He could always recognize it when it was there." *An Evening with Wild Man Fischer* is an unsettling sample of that recognition. It's a rock and roll album conceived as a piece of social anthropology. Fischer's songs suggested simple childlike tunes, but they were also seeped in violence, fantasy, and family dysfunction. Besides studio sessions of Larry telling Zappa his life story and singing his songs, engineer Dick Kunc provided street recordings of Fischer in action on the street. "My first task was to literally follow him around the streets for several days, carrying a Uher two-track, chronicling whatever madness he got into," Kunc recalled.

The second release on Bizarre/Straight was just as unusual. Christine Frka and Pamela Miller were members of a groupie clan that was designated the Laurel Canyon Ballet Company. This gathering included Miss Sandra, Miss Cinderella, and Miss Mercy. While they were visiting the Zappa house, he suggested that they come up with some material for an album. Encouraged, they put together a number of songs about their lifestyle and named themselves the GTO's (Girls Together Outrageously). "I thought it would be interesting to share their experiences with people who had never come in contact with anything like that," Zappa explained. "So I encouraged them to set music to their songs or get somebody to help them put their poems to music and I would record them." *Permanent Damage* was an alluring documentary sample of that lifestyle. Since Zappa treats subject matter, dialogue, and song as musical material, *Permanent Damage* has a casual off-color quality.

Permanent Damage and *An Evening with Wild Man Fischer* were works of oddball sociology as much as they were rock and roll records. Zappa set out to produce albums freely documenting unexplored folkloric aspects of American culture. He went after folks who were both frowned upon by cultural imprimaturs and rejected as outcasts considered not talented enough to be making records. Other new releases on Bizarre/Straight were only slightly less peculiar: Alice Cooper (*Pretties for You*), a psychedelic band that would find fame a few years later; folk singers Tim Dawe (*Penrod*), Tim Buckley (*Blue Afternoon*), and Judy Henske and Jerry Yester (*Farewell Aldebaran*). Zappa had a particular interest in 50s hipster jazz poet Lord Buckley, whose influence on Lenny Bruce didn't go unnoticed. *A Most Immaculately Hip Aristocrat* contained six performance pieces originally recorded in 1956 by Lyle Griffen, which Zappa edited for the album. It was in the early winter of 1968, at a Kentucky Fried Chicken in Los Angeles, just as Zappa was beginning to sign his roster of optionally alternate entertainment to the Bizarre/ Straight label, where he and Beefheart talked about working together.

While Zappa clearly wanted to give Don Van Vliet an opportunity to make his best music, free of the restrictions imposed upon him by bad advice and contract problems, they just didn't mix together very well. "Both Frank and Don had two very extreme personalities, and how they ever did anything together is a mystery to me," Don Preston of the Mothers observed. Beefheart was essentially a musical primitive. His integration of free jazz, Delta blues, absurdism, and idiosyncratic verse was an instinctual choice. Zappa mixed his own musical colors with a deliberate intent. "Van Vliet drew on the paradox of ordered disorder exploited by Hugo Ball in his sound poetry, together with the 'primitivism' of [Tristan] Tzara, rendered urgently audible in the free jazz of Ornette Coleman," wrote Michel Delville and Andrew Norris in *Frank Zappa, Captain Beefheart and the Secret History of Maximalism*. "While Zappa fell in love with the materiality of sound, and the theatrical extravagances of burlesque, key components in his self-recharging brand of social satire . . . Van Vliet played with the paradox, evolving his own surrealist slant on those odd overdetermined objects so dear to Zappa, the latter branched out and out into parody, satire and beyond." The blending of their sensibilities would make for a rare masterpiece in *Trout Mask*

Replica, but it would also secure constant strife in their working relationship.

Some time before their reunion, Beefheart had moved the remaining *Strictly Personal* band into a house on Entrada Drive in Woodland Hills just outside the San Fernando Valley. The place itself had two bedrooms—one for Beefheart and a tiny one for the rest of the group. The living room was set up for rehearsals. The back yard had a large tropical garden and a small bridge featured on the back cover of *Trout Mask*. From there, Beefheart began to recruit new members. To replace Jerry Handley, he turned to his old friend and engineer Gary Marker, who proved to be a sufficient bass player in the Rising Sons. As for Alex Snouffer's replacement, Beefheart brought in a young protegé named Bill Harkleroad. Harkleroad had grown up in Southern California, where (like many California boys before him) he played surf music. But in 1964, after a year of twanging guitar work, he heard Wolfman Jack on XERB playing Howlin' Wolf and BB King, and from there Harkleroad became a blues fanatic.

One of his friends, P.G. Blakely, who played drums on "Diddy Wah Diddy," invited Harkleroad to jam with the Magic Band in 1967. He may have only been eighteen at the time, but he was determined to fit in with the rest of them. "Like most kids I thought I was real hot because I knew about seven licks," Harkleroad recalled. Although he caught the attention of the other bandmembers, Harkleroad went instead to Lake Tahoe to do Jimi Hendrix covers with his new group. While in Lake Tahoe, he encountered a cult called the Brotherhood, which worshipped Timothy Leary, gleaned the psychedelic Zen prayer books of Alan Watts, and devoured copious tabs of LSD. He was happily blissed out on acid the day the call came to audition for the Magic Band after their aborted tour in June 1968. Shortly after the audition, the group headed off to Frank Zappa's house in Laurel Canyon for a huge jam session featuring Mick Jagger, Marianne Faithfull, and Pete Townshend. After a fun evening playing blues and 50s rock and roll, it was decided that Beefheart would re-record the *Strictly Personal* album. That fall, in 1968, Beefheart and Zappa talked about laying down some tracks at Sunset Sound in Hollywood. What may have started as the rehabilitation of *Strictly Personal*, though, soon became the strictly personal odyssey of *Trout Mask Replica*.

Chapter Four
A Little Paranoia Is a Good Propeller

A perfect writer would make words sing, dance, kiss, do the male and female act, bear children, weep, bleed, rage, stab, steal, fire cannon, steer ships, sack cities, charge with cavalry or infantry, or do any thing, that man or woman or the natural powers can do.

—Walt Whitman, "The Renovated English Speech," *An American Primer*, 1904

When you listen to Beefheart's voice on *Trout Mask Replica*, it doesn't define itself as clearly as other blues or rock singers. Some people say they hear Howlin' Wolf in the lascivious growl of Beefheart's tenor. Others insist on hearing the raucous spirit of Richard Berry—not the Berry of "Louie Louie," mind you, but rather the sly narrator of the Robins' hit "Riot on Cell Block #9." Occasionally, a few detect a little of Muddy Waters, a pinch of the attitude of Charley Patton, perhaps the rhythms of Robert Pete Williams. Not bad company and not entirely wrong. But Beefheart isn't so much an inheritor as he is inhabited. He doesn't suggest influences; he demonstrates pure possession. "I was never influenced," he insisted. "Possessed, but never influenced." Which is why when I listen to Beefheart, the voice of Texas-born blues singer Blind Willie Johnson comes immediately to mind. Johnson's voice, possessed of an unearthly power, holds an unfathomable mystery in its texture. So does Don Van Vliet's.

Born in 1897 in Brenham, Texas, Johnson was blinded at the age of seven when, according to legend, his mother threw lye in his face to avenge a beating from his father. Undaunted, he still taught himself to play a distinctive bottleneck guitar. Johnson performed at Baptist Association meetings and churches, where he quickly came to see the light. Much has been written about Johnson's accomplished guitar style, probably the most influential in blues history, but less ink has been devoted to his voice. In a series of recordings he made for Columbia Records between 1927 and 1930, Johnson recorded nothing but religious songs, but he stripped them of all piety. His style was paradoxical. He sang with an intensity known only to the blues, but he mixed it with Pentecostal fire. Johnson had a raspy tenor that could take flight, lose control, and then ride out the contours of the space his voice opened up around him. The force of that voice was so great that he was once arrested in New Orleans for causing a riot. By singing his Samson and Delilah story, "If I Had My Way I'd Tear This Building Down," some people were inspired to almost act on it.

In song after song, Johnson told biblical tales, from "Jesus Make Up My Dying Bed" to "John the Revelator," posing as many questions as he offered answers. Each track spoke apocalyptic fire while offering up riddles and unending spiritual quests. Each song plumbed the depths of an eternal question that Johnson would ask explicitly in "Soul of a Man" ("I want somebody to tell me / Just what is the soul of man?"). The question was basic, but Johnson's query had a sense of urgent drama suggesting that this knowledge wasn't enough. Whether it was "God Moves on the Water," adapted to address the fate of the Titanic, or "Can't Nobody Hide from God," which was later turned loose on America's enemies during World War II, Johnson's songs tore up the soul as much as they sought its definition. In "Dark Was the Night (Cold Was the Ground)," the ultimate story of the crucifixion, he didn't use words. Over the slow whine of his guitar, Johnson quietly moans and wails the dark mystery of Jesus's last night on the cross, as if singing lyrics would diminish that fateful event. He knew the story so intimately that, perhaps approximating his own blindness, he deprived us of a language to explain it. Yet without words, the song became cryptic, eerie, and otherworldly to experience. You began to think that Johnson wasn't just depicting the death of Christ, but addressing His eternal question of the Heavenly Father: *Why dost thou forsake me?* That part of the riddle was clearly felt—if not understood—by all who heard it. On the Voyager 1, launched by NASA in 1977, among collections of ancient chants, sound effects, and sublime recordings by Bach and Beethoven, astronomer Carl Sagan wisely included Blind Willie Johnson's dramatic reading of the crucifixion. Someday Johnson's enigmatic story may be heard by some extraterrestrial life curiously encountering that space probe. Maybe they'll even wonder, as they listen intently, just what is the soul of man?

Although many of Blind Willie Johnson's songs eventually found earthly homes in the catalogue of Led Zeppelin ("Nobody's Fault but Mine," "In My Time of Dying"), Eric Clapton ("Motherless Children"), and Ry Cooder (*Paris, Texas*), the actual spirit of Blind Willie Johnson, for me, is clearest in Captain Beefheart. Although Beefheart is not on the same spiritual crusade as Johnson, he, too, strips the human voice of all natural affectation to reach for its bottom end, its very core. There's no room for influence in both Blind Willie and Beefheart. Everything is pared down to the essence of their voices, their pure freedom in stating exactly who they are—to testify. That's what happens on "Moonlight on Vermont," the first recorded track that would ultimately appear on *Trout Mask Replica*.

While the original plan at Sunset Sound that fall was to rerecord *Strictly Personal*, Beefheart began to push toward laying down some new tracks. The lineup now featured Jeff Cotton and Bill Harkleroad on guitars, Gary Marker on bass, and John French on drums. The first new song, "Moonlight on Vermont," had its origins in the 1943 song "Moonlight in Vermont," which was a quaintly romantic ballad by John Blackburn and Karl Suessdorf. Many singers, including Margaret Whiting, Ray Charles, and Johnny Mathis, rendered its pastoral lyricism ("Pennies in a stream / Falling leaves a sycamore / Moonlight in Vermont") into hit songs over the years. Perhaps the most famous being Frank Sinatra on his 1958 album, *Come Fly with Me.* Given Beefheart's strong advocacy of nature, "Moonlight in Vermont" became the perfect template for a far more intense exotic tale. But he tells the story of "Moonlight in Vermont" by way of Howlin' Wolf's "Moanin' at Midnight."

Unlike Blackburn and Suessdorf, Beefheart has a far different reading of the stormy power of nature. In "Moonlight in Vermont," set in an American state about as white as the winter snow, nature is a calmly seductive force out of a William Wordsworth poem ("Ev'ning summer breeze / Warbling of a meadowlark / Moonlight in Vermont"). Beefheart brings the religious fervour of Blind Willie Johnson into creating a far more erotic parable of lust and the sensual power of the phases of the moon. The song begins with the Vermont moonlight casting a strange spell on the prosaic Mrs. Wooten, and her son, Little Nitty, who gets an erection ("Even lifebuoy floatin' / With his lil' pistol showin' / 'N his little pistol totin'"). "Moonlight on Vermont" doesn't view nature as a harmonizing force—it incites. As Beefheart explains in the chorus, "That goes t' show you what uh moon can do!"

"Human beings are not nature's favorites," Camille Paglia writes in *Sexual Personae*, her powerfully insightful study of sex and nature. "We are merely one of a multitude of species upon which nature indiscriminately exerts its force. Nature has a master agenda we can only dimly know." It is the mystery of that master agenda that takes the holiness out of Blind Willie Johnson's biblical tales. Revelation wasn't a Sunday School story for Johnson, it was a powerful and puzzling transformation that could shake foundations. Nature deals a Dionysian card in

Beefheart's song, where now there's "no more bridge from Tuesday t' Friday / Everybody's gone high society." The pun on Cole Porter's "High Society," on the favoured station of the social classes, is also a contemporary definition of a 60s pagan society clouded in marijuana smoke.

The moon inspires the luckless white elephant to escape from the zoo, its proverbial prison, finding peanuts now littering the curb. (In the booklet accompanying the Mothers' *Uncle Meat* album, Zappa includes a drawing of a toy giraffe happily listening to "Moonlight on Vermont" on the radio, just as a doll's foot is about to sexually penetrate it from behind.) In the song, it's the moon that brings on an eruption, the celebration of life's broad diversity. Ultimately, it gets Beefheart invoking "Ol' Time Religion." "It was good for Aphrodite / She's a mighty righteous sighty / and her Priestess wears no nightie / And that's good enough for me," wails Beefheart as he links the primal power of God, beauty, and sex. "If Picasso wanted to paint like a child, Van Vliet wants to paint like an animal," Michel Delville and Andrew Norris wrote in *Frank Zappa, Captain Beefheart and the Secret History of Maximalism*. In fact, Beefheart delivers the child to its animal nature and celebrates it in "Moonlight on Vermont."

In telling his wild tale, Beefheart naturally falls back on the blues. It opens with an infernal kick from John French's drums that's answered by the powerhouse intensity of Harkleroad's guitar ("a screeching Telecaster part played way up the neck with a capo through this Showman amp that was as big as a hotel," Harkleroad recalled). What we get to hear blows fire: an abstract gospel blues with an added touch inspired by avant-garde composer Steve

Reich's "Come Out." In "Come Out," Reich had sampled, within his score, an evangelist's fire and brimstone sermon. According to Pamela Des Barres of the GTO's, the members of the groupie band came around to Beefheart's house to smoke some weed and get any eyeful of John French. While there, Beefheart played Reich's opus for them and they became so mesmerized that they let the record continue to skip over the repeated phrase—"come out to show them."

"Moonlight on Vermont" contains a foreboding sound that can wake the dead—as it did for one fan of *Trout Mask Replica*, writing on amazon.com. He encountered the song's force quite unconsciously when he left his multiple CD player on as he fell asleep—with *Trout Mask* on deck. When it began to play, his sleep was rudely interrupted by the urgency of "Moonlight on Vermont." "Upon waking, my first thought was 'my God there's a war going on,'" he wrote. "I scrambled for the light and for the remote, but after finding the remote, I couldn't turn it off because I was captivated. While [it sounded] chaotic, it seemed to make sense." That was the true incongruity of this song: a chaos out of Armageddon that eventually comes to make sense.

Another new song they recorded, which would conclude *Trout Mask Replica*, was "Veteran's Day Poppy," an antiwar song told from the point of view of a father who has just lost his son in battle. Lamenting the significance of the poppy, in the face of the familial loss, Beefheart exclaims, "It can never grow another son / Like the one who warmed me my days." While lyrically the track is—for Beefheart—fairly straightforward, the title is a playful double-entendre (*Poppy* is also *Papa*). "Suffice to say that one of

Don's favorite words was 'juxtaposition,'" Harkleroad explained. Yet even if the lyric is simple, "Veteran's Day Poppy" is musically dense, with an intricate coda at the end. "That section at the end was obviously tacked on later," Harkleroad told Billy James in *Lunar Notes*. "Zappa showed me this major 7th chord—actually it comes out as a minor 9th—but I didn't know about relative major-minor stuff then. If you listen to the end section it's kind of Zappa-like." Mike Barnes also rightly asserts that the slide guitar in the opening is lifted from the popular 40s song, "Rancho Grande."

The only track they rerecorded from *Strictly Personal* was "Kandy Korn," but it never got completed. Before the sessions completed, Gary Marker started to sense a portentous dynamic emerging in the studio, which bore significance further down the road. There was a growing competitive tension developing between Zappa and Beefheart. "The real operative current in the studio that night was the competition between Zappa and Don," Marker told Mike Barnes. "If there's any tension in that stuff, it's there." Often it was instigated by Zappa, too, who would taunt Beefheart to do bird whistles until he would ultimately relent. The tension didn't escalate, however, since the recordings were pretty close to completion. During the early winter of 1969, Zappa prepared to head out on the road for what would turn out to be his final tour with that current edition of the Mothers. Beefheart, meanwhile, took the Magic Band back to their house and mapped out the new music for his upcoming record.

The first task, though, was to find a permanent bass player, since Gary Marker made it clear that his inclusion was only temporary. Mark Boston had once played bass in one of Harkleroad's blues cover groups, so he was invited to join up. "When I joined, I thought I was gonna be playing blues," Boston explained to *Mojo* magazine in 2005. His assumption wasn't misplaced, because he had last seen the Magic Band back at the Teenage Fair, when they were still *playing* the blues. Despite concerns that he might not fit in, Boston ultimately won over the group. One new member who didn't immediately win over everyone (except Beefheart) was Victor Hayden. Although Beefheart added Hayden on bass clarinet, the problem was, he couldn't actually play it. "He was totally untrained, completely," French told Bryon Coley of *Spin*. "He hadn't even played a horn before. It was just basically squawking around a bit." Harkleroad was even less charitable. "I'm not sure I would say that he played it, so much as pushed air through it," Harkleroad added.

Besides being Beefheart's cousin, what likely interested Vliet most about including Hayden in the group was the atypical aspect of having someone who *could* only "push air" and "squawk" through bass clarinet. Out of the failure to realize *Brown Wrapper*, plus the mess that became *Strictly Personal*, Beefheart envisioned a music with a purity of sound, not harmony and melody. He knew he would need the most unorthodox (and dedicated) band to accomplish it. The first step in this new direction was to rename the members (as Zappa had once renamed him). Mark Boston became Rockette Morton, Jeff Cotton was christened Antennae Jimmy Semens, Victor Hayden was the Mascara Snake, John French inherited the obvious moniker Drumbo, and Bill Harkleroad became Zoot Horn Rollo. Harkleroad wasn't so sure he liked the name at first, but eventually grew to accept it. "I guess the name fit in with this strange music we were playing and in time I felt very comfortable with it, and still do," Harkleroad explained.

As for the "strange music," which would ultimately comprise *Trout Mask Replica*, the inspiration for it was partly due to the jazz records that Gary Marker had been playing Beefheart over the past couple of years. Among the stacks of Archie Shepp, John Coltrane, and Charles Lloyd albums, there was one record that particularly stood out. It was a rare disc by author Lawrence Lipton called *Jazz Canto*. Lipton was a writer with a varied career, who early in the 40s wrote mysteries, novels, and poetry. In the late 50s, when he was in his sixties, he became linked to the Beat writers such as Jack Keroauc and Allen Ginsberg in the poetry renaissance in San Francisco. Later that year, Lipton began experimenting with the latent musical rhythms within verse by combining poetry with jazz music. While working with Shelly Manne, Jimmie Giuffre, and Buddy Colette, he perfected an integration of the two forms. When Benny Carter and Jack Hampton heard Lipton discussing his fusion of poetry and jazz on CBS Radio, they called on him to produce a whole series of poetry and jazz concerts. This not only led to the First West Coast Poetry and Jazz Festival in December 1957, it resulted the following year in a concept record for World Pacific Records called *Jazz Canto*. The album drew upon the musical talents of Shorty Rogers, Paul Horn, and Barney Kessel to shape their music around the recitations of poets like Kenneth Rexroth, Stuart Z. Perkoff, and many other West Coast bohemians. The record provided a portal by which Beefheart could combine poetic timbre with the musical arrangements from his group.

Gary Marker had also partly provided the idea for the musical structure of *Trout Mask*. One day, while learning how to edit, Marker was told to take out a number of reference tapes and put together a series of four-bar and eight-bar segments in a random order, then match them up so that the metre would be accurate. While Marker was playing back his seemlessly edited opus of disjointed parts, Beefheart happened to enter the studio and immediately wanted to know what he was doing. Once Marker explained the process to him, Don decided that he wanted to create a music that was, as Marker recalled, "like punching buttons on a radio and getting random stuff that hangs together." To achieve this conceptual strategy for *Trout Mask Replica*, Beefheart turned to the one person he could: John French. "Alex [Snouffer] directed the original band, until Don kept asserting himself to the point where Alex became disgusted and gave up," French explained to Bryon Coley of *Spin*. "It took somebody to arrange what Don was doing; not creating music necessarily—although I created a lot of my own drum parts—but just making sure that everybody knows what everything is, so that the tunes don't go on for twenty minutes."

The popular myth, devised by Beefheart, then embellished by the rock press, was that he composed all the songs on *Trout Mask Replica* at a piano in a remarkable eight-day span. Not only is the claim patently false, it helped propagate a cult of personality around Beefheart. It was reminiscent of the declarations made by many auteur film critics that Orson Welles was the sole genius behind

Citizen Kane, as if Herman J. Mankiewicz's screenplay were merely an adjunct to the picture. Yet the *Trout Mask* myth served another purpose. It enabled Beefheart to claim an artistic control thus far denied him, and it pitted him as the resident genius next to his friend/rival Frank Zappa. Since most rock critics despised Zappa, especially for his snide put-downs of the counterculture scene, it proved easier to exalt the more romantic view of Beefheart as the misunderstood master. It's a spurious perspective still held today —although the Magic Band has finally been recognized for the importance of their contributions.

One significant truth of Beefheart's assertion, though, was that he began composing the music for *Trout Mask* on the piano. One day, he brought one into the house, even though (in the spirit of Victor Hayden) he couldn't play it. As Mike Barnes pointed out in his Beefheart biography, Vliet approached the piano in an intuitive manner, "unencumbered by technique as he possessed none." Barnes described the process, quoting future Magic Band guitarist Gary Lucas, by suggesting that Beefheart was "throwing a pack of cards in the air, photographing them as they fell and then getting the . . . musicians to reproduce the frozen moment." John French agreed with the intuitive approach Beefheart applied. "Don could neither read nor write music notation as he had no formal music education," he explained. "Yet with this handicap, he still managed to communicate several albums worth of material through whistling, singing, and playing parts on guitars, drums, harmonicas, pianos, and any other instrument within reach. Had he been able to write music in the conventional manner, there is no telling what this man might have accomplished musically."

Even so, Beefheart accomplished more than anyone could have bargained for—and French knew it. This is one reason why he used a tape recorder to get Beefheart's spontaneous musical lines down for notation. "I had been tape recording Don's piano parts," French remembered. "He would go on for hours, just hours, to get one little thing on there and we finally ran out of tape. He was like, 'John, record this! Get this, man! Get this! Come on!' He'd be sitting at the piano, trapped in his own creativity, because he couldn't get up. If he moved his hands he'd forget what he was doing." Harkleroad had vivid recollections of watching the two men in process. "There were days and days when [Beefheart] and John French were pounding out parts. I don't mean to diminish [Beefheart]'s creativity or his view of the big picture, but he would play something and couldn't repeat it ten minutes later. . . . John would try to make him do that so he could write it. [Beefheart] was chiselling away at rhythmic shapes and sounds, and it wasn't done in any concise way where he had a direct vision of what he was going to come up with, other than the parts that the band was going to put together." Soon the process broke down when French accidently erased a tape they'd made. "I'd be looking for tapes through these old reel-to-reel tapes," French said. "I'd drop one on the floor and it would roll away and unspool. . . . I couldn't find any tape, so one day I just took the fuse out of the tape recorder and said it was broken. 'Won't work anymore.'"

French quickly decided to bring some manuscript paper to their sessions and began writing drum patterns to Beefheart's whistled, or vocalized, musical phrases. He would write the notation and play it back to him. "I had a spiral-bound music manuscript book and one day I attempted to transcribe something as Don played," French remembered. "Pitches were a little rough at first, but I knew rhythms well. After writing a couple of passages, I unconsciously laid the book down and walked out of the room. Don approached me later, downstairs, and, displaying the transcription, asked, 'Can you play this back?' I said, 'I'll give it a try!' After a moderately successful replay, this became the method by which much of *Trout Mask Replica* was written." For hours, they would sit there working out their strategy, coming up with the notations for "Dali's Car," an instrumental that would later appear on *Trout Mask*. "He did not think in long passages," French explained. "Most of his passages were fairly short, just a bunch of riffs put together. And he couldn't play from one to the other. The music works, but to me it's rhythmically random. And it wasn't done because Don was thinking, intentionally, 'Oh, here I'll go into 3/4.' He never thought about key signatures. He never thought about time signatures. You could say, 'Don, where's middle C?' And he wouldn't know. He had no idea about that. That doesn't stop someone from being a creative person, but it definitely stops them from being able to communicate what it is they want to do." The job of communicating this new music to the rest of the group fell to French.

"John would show us the parts," Harkleroad recalled. "[H]e had a tremendous amount of control over who played what. Don didn't know what we were playing. As he heard us rehearsing the songs—and he rarely was at rehearsals—he would become familiar with the parts we were working out, and he might say, 'That's great,' or 'You

need to fix that.' But the way we'd play in different time signatures and make it work together—how we would come
together after twelve beats and then move on to the next
section—wasn't determined by Don." If the musical end
was pretty much the combined effort of the Magic Band,
the lyrics were all Beefheart. "The lyric was onto itself and
the music was unto itself, and they were crammed together, sometimes magically and other times not so well,"
Harkleroad explained. "There was never any rehearsing of
the lyrics, so they were very separate." For the band,
Beefheart was using these chunks of musical sound much
the way a sculptor shapes clay. "He adopted more of the
mentality of a sculptor," Harkleroad explained. "His idea
was to use sound, bodies, and people as tools. It was
increasingly clear that our job as his band was to turn it
into sounds that were repeatable."

For much of the late autumn of 1968, into the early winter of 1969, the group rehearsed the music endlessly until
Zappa returned from his tour to begin producing the
record. However, as nourished as they were by playing this
new music, they were literally starving. "We were all totally
broke," French explained. "There was no money. Basically
Don's mother was supporting the band and [Harkleroad's]
mother would send down cheques to pay the rent and buy
food. I remember once going for a month and all we had to
eat every day was one little ration of a four-ounce cup of
soya beans." The group was in fact so poor they even resort-
ed to stealing food. One time, they actually got caught.
Before heading out on the tour, Zappa bailed them out of
jail. "I remember waking up in the middle of the night,"
French remembered. "I could hear everybody sleeping, so I

crawled into the kitchen on my hands and knees, very very quietly. I took a piece of bread . . . I lay with my head under my blanket, munching on this bread, like it was a feast. . . . I actually remember one time drinking pancake syrup. I was so hungry I just poured it in a glass and drank it. I had to have something in my stomach."

Beefheart drove the musicians hard, making them play twelve to fourteen hours a day. He was "conditioning" the band by keeping them talking for up to thirty-six hours straight. "When I first joined the group, Don was going to the library looking up books on how to control people, and literally how to brainwash these young kids," Harkleroad recalled. "We're talking sleep deprivation, food deprivation." Working so close to Beefheart, French saw how Don would use the same underhanded techniques to gain control that he used to get Doug Moon out of the group. "We'd have these, what I used to call, 'brainwashing sessions,' where he'd decide someone in the band was Public Enemy #1. He'd centre in on them for two or three days, feed them coffee and not let them sleep until their sense of deprivation was such that they'd say, 'I'll do anything you say!' Then they'd fall apart and cry or something . . . it was very emotionally disturbing to all of us and it took us a long time to get past that." The band never saw anyone outside the house—in fact, they rarely left the residence. Just prior to recording *Trout Mask*, French, Jeff Cotton, and Mark Boston tried to escape in the middle of the night. Boston even had his clothes hidden across the road in a field. Often Vliet would make emotional appeals for them to stay.

Beefheart once said that paranoia was a good propeller.

He used it here to instill fear in the group, grinding the band into his own personal sounding board and, eventually, earning their loyalty. Sometimes he would do spontaneous readings of his lyrics looking specifically for some response. At the end of "Old Fart at Play," for example, you can hear an excerpt from one of those sessions where Jeff Cotton (Antennae Jimmy Semens) is heard saying, "Oh man, that's so heavy!" He would play cultural impresario, introducing them to the works of various contemporary artists like Robert Rauschenberg and Willem De Kooning, sometimes talking endlessly about Monet, or regaling them about the passion he felt for the work of Modigliani. Despite the cultlike atmosphere, with a tyrant now in charge, the music the group played was itself strangely liberating. "Those tunes became magical to my ears—they felt like a part of me," Harkleroad wrote in *Lunar Notes*. "It was all so new and I felt I was participating in something that defied description." By the time Zappa returned to Los Angeles in the spring, the group was ready to begin defying reality.

Chapter Five
Music from the Other Side
of the Fence

You can physically drown in paint, you can mentally drown in music.

—Don Van Vliet

The quest for pure freedom that *Trout Mask Replica* sought came out of nowhere in the world of rock and roll. The ground it travelled, however, had already been tilled in the other arts. For example, its roots lay in abstract expressionism, where painters applied their paint gesturally and nongeometrically to the canvas with speed and force, to convey depth of emotion through sensation. The pure spontaneity in the work of Franz Kline, Hans Hoffman, Jean Dubuffet, Willem de Kooning, and especially Jackson Pollock, cut through the limits of realism by suggesting that the expressive method of painting was just as valuable as the painting itself. As a movement, originating in the 40s, it would soon become fiercely popular in the visual arts world of the 50s.

At the turn of the twentieth century, a number of classical composers were growing weary of tonality and wishing to dispense with the adherence to a single key as the one accepted foundation for musical composition. In response, Arnold Schoenberg developed a twelve-tone system in which all twelve notes in the chromatic scale were performed before the initial note was played again. Anton Webern offered his own interpretation of twelve-tone serialism by using it to create an abstract sparseness in his pieces. Igor Stravinsky became inspired to take music back to a pre-romantic era. From there, he could explore form rather than content, ultimately leading him into neoclassicism and interpreting the music of the past. Composer Edgard Varèse wished to clear the decks altogether by reinventing western music at its core. He explored it as a scientific construct of sounds, creating a whole new world of music yet unheard.

As for American jazz music, many of its practitioners already considered it free, built on improvisation, soloing, and liberated voices calling out to one another. But by the 50s, there were some who claimed it wasn't free enough. "Free jazz" became a radical deviation from the form that challenged the conventional chord progressions and time signatures at its foundation. It erupted out of the untimely death of Charlie Parker, who opened the door for innovators to rethink the legacy they inherited. Pianist Cecil Taylor, for instance, decided to bring the ideas of Schoenberg and Webern into the land of Bud Powell and Horace Silver. In 1957, he appeared at the Newport Jazz Festival with an abstract atonal sound that, as he put it, "imitate[s] on the piano the leaps in space a dancer makes." Those leaps began in a lonely loft where by night, after returning from his dull day job delivering sandwiches, he would hold "imaginary concerts" of his music, envisioning an audience that could one day hear and appreciate it.

Ornette Coleman, a Texas-born saxophone player who eventually sojourned to LA, took his own leaps into space with his quartet by playing jazz music that abandoned form altogether. When he appeared at the Five Spot nightclub in New York in the early winter of 1959, he inspired a small riot resembling the larger one Stravinsky had instigated in 1913 with *Le Sacre du Printemps*. "It was like I was E.T. or something, just dropped in from the moon," Coleman remembered. He achieved extraterrestrial status by abandoning harmony. Coleman sought rhythm the way abstract expressionist painters went after sensation through dazzling speed. Melody was experienced through a musical maze, an acceleration of tempo, demanding that the audience follow along as he abandoned jazz's adherence to strict time. Naturally, Coleman's music became a favorite of painter Jackson Pollock, who provided a canvas of exploding color for the cover of the self-explanatory *Free Jazz* (1960).

While all these tributaries fed into the river that baptised Don Van Vliet, one significant stream was the work of John Coltrane. While stylistically Beefheart is closer to the work of Cecil Taylor, Ornette Coleman, and the abstract expressionists, he cuts through the blues with the same sharp precision that Coltrane cut through jazz. This is by no means comparing the primitive talent of Beefheart with the pure genius of Coltrane, but both men were pioneers of a similar cause. For twenty years, between 1947 and 1967, Coltrane played saxophone engrossed with a desire to reach a place yet unheard, unfelt, and spiritually solvent. Beginning his career with a desire to be "consumed" by the spirit of Charlie Parker, in actuality, he was consumed in the early years by drugs and alcohol. One day, he had a spiritual awakening through vegetarianism and eastern religion, which lead him on a quest "to make others happy through music."

His career had begun with Dizzy Gillespie's band in the late 40s, until Coltrane hooked up with trumpeter Miles Davis in the mid-50s, when he began to hone a virtuosity in improvisation. They were an audacious contrast in styles. Where Davis was a master of spareness, Coltrane could never seem to cram enough notes into a bar of music. His heroin problem got him kicked out of Davis's group, but then he began a short term with pianist Thelonious Monk before kicking his habit permanently. Coltrane had found a mentor in Monk. Monk taught him methods of creating complex harmonic structures within his sax solos, which in time would be long, difficult excursions into abstract blues. Coltrane could take a conventional pop song, like Rodgers and Hammerstein's "My Favorite Things" in 1960, and enlarge the melody on soprano saxophone by building an extended solo overtop the basic chords of the theme. Within a year, though, in a series of concerts at the Village Vanguard, Coltrane used melody as merely a starting place for epic solos that built in intensity like a chainsaw cutting through a tornado. Sometimes they would last close to an hour. "Chasin' the Trane," for example, featured over eighty choruses that were built upon a twelve-bar blues. That intensity would reach a spiritual epiphany in 1964 with the luxuriant devotional suite *A Love Supreme*. Like Blind Willie Johnson years earlier, Coltrane was possessed by a higher power and a purpose that was expressed through a fervent desire to remake himself through his art. "My music is the spiritual expression of what I am—my faith, my knowledge, my being," Coltrane remarked.

Where many would take the path of sanctimony, Coltrane sought out dissonance rather than harmony. It reached its zenith a year later in Seattle in 1965. That year, he was recording a phenomenal amount of music, each piece becoming more abstract than the last. One night, he had a dream in which he and the band had played a show without reference to chords or chordal sequences. In his dream, he discovered that he was seeking, in the words of jazz critic Keith Raether in *Earshot Jazz,* "dialogues of tonal and atonal sections similar to the parallel octave passages found in African vocal music." The sessions Coltrane recorded after his dream were the kind that could cause others to have nightmares. "We did two takes and both had that kind of thing in them that makes people scream," saxophonist Marion Brown explained. During the concert in Seattle, Coltrane decided to take his group, which also included Pharoah Sanders on sax, Elvin Jones on drums, and Jimmy Garrison on bass, through the most atonal abstractions he'd ever played. The purpose? "I don't think I'll know what's missing from my playing until I find it," Coltrane told a journalist from *Melody Maker* before the show. One of the tracks, "Evolution," was a thirty-six-minute excursion into an extravagant sheet of combative chords that filled close to two sides of an LP. The Harold Arlen standard "Out of This World" became literally that. It was so dense in atonality that the recording engineer, Jan Kurtis, who knew Coltrane's original recording of the song, didn't recognize it until well into the piece. In what became an understatement of perception, Kurtis told Keith Raether:

"Coltrane seemed to be thinking about a lot of things. There must have been an enormous amount of music going on inside him."

The enormity of that music was overwhelming for most people to consume. When a friend of mine, who loves Coltrane, bought a used CD of *John Coltrane: Live in Seattle* (on my recommendation), he phoned me shortly after hearing only a portion of it. "I'm taking this back," he cried. Somewhat puzzled, I asked him why. He replied pejoratively, "This is. . . . Beefheart!" He had heard in Coltrane what he once perceived briefly in *Trout Mask*. At that moment, I suddenly recalled playing him about twenty-five seconds of the record (before he begged me to turn it off). By Seattle, Coltrane had dispensed of conventional melodies in his own search for what Blind Willie Johnson had been looking for in his gospel blues: the soul of a man. For both men, the soul of a man was not a harmonious place. So the octane Coltrane provided was pure force, a streaming of notes too primal to contain, a musical speaking in tongues, so to speak. For my friend, of course, it was much less than that. It was tongues that were garbled, pure noise, no more than an unlistenable cacophony. Music from the other side of the fence. When Beefheart released *Trout Mask Replica*, it was spawned from the same type of spiritual hermitage that took Coltrane to Seattle four years earlier.

Although *Trout Mask Replica* has its antecedents in all these varied sources, it has none in the world of rock. That is partly due to the fact that—unlike the visual arts, classical music, and jazz—rock is a populist music. Classical music and jazz, arguably, have a comparatively minority audience. "Pop music provides immediate emotional gratifications that the subtler and deeper and more lasting pleasures of jazz can't prevail against," film critic Pauline Kael once wrote in her ambivalent praise of *Lady Sings the Blues*, the movie biography of singer Billie Holiday. "Pop drives jazz back underground," she explained. It's in that underground, though, where a laboratory of experimentation can flourish. Since the huge dollars and the mass audience don't drive that world, lone dreamers (like Cecil Taylor) could endlessly perform their imaginary concerts. That underground made these distinct kinds of propulsive forces possible, in a way that they never could in rock and roll. The stage that Elvis Presley and the Beatles built, as big and as bold as it was, couldn't break totally free from the huge business that ultimately needed to make money from its art. This is why the emergence of *Trout Mask Replica* seemed so abhorrent when it hit the record stores in 1969. Who the fuck would want to listen to this? It's Beefheart!

* * *

By the late winter of 1969, when Beefheart and the group were ready to begin recording their album, Frank Zappa already had an idea of how he wanted to produce it. During the road tour with the Mothers, he had been recording their live gigs with an ingeniously inexpensive unit. Sound engineer Dick Kunc had a Shure eight-channel mixer mounted in a portable briefcase. At all performances, Kunc would simply sit in a corner and adjust levels through his headphones, whereby he could monitor the band through the briefcase mixer that was feeding a portable state-of-the-art Uher reel-to-reel recorder. "It was a tough little machine and it made spectacular recordings," Kunc said. "Sometimes I used just the single stereo microphone that came with it; other times I set up four separate mics or so and fed them to the Uher." Since the road tapes turned out so well, Zappa figured it might also work for recording *Trout Mask*. "I thought it would be great to go to Don's house with this portable rig and put the drums in the bedroom, the bass clarinet in the kitchen, and the vocals in the bathroom, complete isolation just like in a studio—except that the band members probably would feel more at home, since they were at home," he wrote in *The Real Frank Zappa Book*. Zappa approached the album as an anthropological field recording—just as he had done with *An Evening with Wild Man Fischer*. He treated the band's home as their own organic recording studio. "I think it's a valid way to approach what we were doing, because who lives in a house for nine months, playing twelve, fourteen hours a day these same tunes?" explained Bill Harkleroad to Alex Duke and Rob DeNunzio of the internet site the Captain Beefheart Radar Station.

Once they got rolling, the sessions began very casually, as if Zappa and Beefheart were once again revisiting that old Webcor in the abandoned classroom. In the beginning, Zappa set up the band (minus Don) and had them play all the songs they had been tirelessly working on. Meanwhile he was instigating a number of theatrical pieces, as well, to include on the record. Most of them involved Mark Boston (including a Rockette Morton routine that precedes "Fallin' Ditch"). But John French wanted none of it. "Frank would occasionally approach me and suggest some zany verbal role which he had undoubtedly spontaneously conceived in a moment of 'inspiration,'" French recalled. "I for the most part ignored him, feeling that this was Don's 'show' and I would be firmly vilified later for allowing myself to be manipulated by Frank at any level."

On the surviving tapes of the house sessions, the mood was pretty upbeat and the only tension was in the anticipation of just what might happen. The first day begins with engineer Dick Kunc trying out the Uher. Once he discovers that everything seems to be working, Bill Harkleroad and Mark Boston begin rigorously practicing the opening notes of the song "Hobo Chang Ba." Kunc then becomes aware of how quickly he will have to ride the levels. There are obvious surprises built into this music. "That's really loud," he says astonishingly while monitoring the playback on his headphones. "You can hear that in there?" Harkleroad asks surprised because his amp isn't even turned on. Don jumps in quickly to warn Kunc that these guitarists just might break the speakers. Kunc then becomes apprehensive, perhaps wondering what speakers he is referring to. "Are we waiting for something?" Kunc asks quietly, not sure now what to expect. "Us," is the answer from Boston, "if it's alright to get a microphone." "Can we play now?" asks Harkleroad impatiently. Kunc is now feeling the kind of confidence he recently gained from the Mothers' tour. He replies, "Yeah. If you want to. Sure." "Alright," Don says eagerly awaiting the results. "What would you like to play?" Kunc asks. Don answers, "'Dachau.'" The amps are turned up as Kunc gets the levels down and the cacophony begins with the first instrumental phrases of the apocalyptic number "Dachau Blues."

After the band struggles through a few moments of "Dachau Blues," they settle into the instrumental "Hair Pie: Bake 2." "Magnificent!" Zappa yells approvingly as the song ends. He sounds assured that this field recording is up to his expectations. Meanwhile French describes to someone the acoustic effect of the corrugated cardboard he has placed on his drum set. Apparently, the neighbour next door was complaining about the noise coming from the group and French tried to soften the sound of his set. "We had this neurotic neighbour who couldn't stand any noise," French remembered. "Every time we started to practice she called the police. We had several visits from the police before I finally put cardboard on my drums." This charitable act ultimately evolved into an artistic strategy by the time they started the final recording sessions—an idea that Zappa wasn't too crazy about. "Usually, when you record a drum set, the cymbals provide part of the 'air' at the top end of the mix," he wrote in *The Real Frank Zappa Book*. "Without a certain amount of this frequency information, mixes tend to sound claustrophobic." Nevertheless, it provided for the percussion its own distinctive quality. Rather than simply keeping the beat, the drums were now as discrete as the other instrumentalists. Once they wrap the first day's recording, Don says, "Jesus!" in response to the wonderful noise he has just heard. Everyone appears to be happy. It sounds like a musical Garden of Eden.

Within days of that recording, Beefheart was taxing the patience of the Garden's residents. It began with the demands he was making on the executives at Bizarre/Straight. While doing these house sessions, he had asked for a tree surgeon to be in residence. Apparently, Beefheart thought the trees around the house might become frightened of all the noise and fall over. "What I remember most of all is a pair of male and female eucalyptus trees," Beefheart explained. "We'd play music to them, and they were really thriving, although they hadn't been when we got there. But it started raining terribly and I was really worried about them. I suddenly decided, 'God, I've got to get something done about this.' So I went out and got eight tree surgeons and we saved those trees." Straight refused Beefheart's request outright, but they still received a bill for $250.

Next, despite everyone's satisfaction with the recordings, Beefheart accused Zappa of being cheap and demanded to bring the band into a studio. "I recall Don had brought Frank into the living room on approximately the third day of recording," French explained. "'Look at them, Frank!' he said. 'They're trapped! They can't transcend their environment!'" The group hardly felt trapped. According to French, they were doing just fine in their home environment. But Beefheart demanded to see studio time, which pretty much jettisoned the idea of the album becoming an anthropological field recording. Quickly, they moved the proceedings to Whitney Studios in Glendale, a studio that Dick Kunc had discovered that was owned by the Mormon church. "They had a monstrous pipe organ with rooms full of pipes and remote instruments," Kunc told Mike Barnes. "The group was certainly well rehearsed . . . and was ready for anything." This became an important factor, since Zappa initially wanted the basic tracks recorded in the house, while saving the studio for Don's vocals. Now he had to provide about six hours of studio time to do twenty tracks, plus the vocals.

Besides the arduous task of accomplishing that feat, Beefheart was creating more headaches for Zappa. "Ordinarily, a singer goes in the studio, puts earphones on, listens to the track, tries to sing in time with it and away you go," Zappa explained. "[But] Don couldn't tolerate the headphones. He wanted to stand in the studio and sing as loud as he could—singing along with the audio leakage coming through the three panes of glass which comprised the control-room window. The chances of him staying in sync was nil —but that's how the vocals were done." Beefheart couldn't fathom what Zappa was so upset about. "I was playing—just like the whales," he told Zig Zag. "I don't think there is such a thing as synchronization . . . that's what they do before a commando raid, isn't it?"

Given what he was faced with, Zappa probably would have preferred a commando raid. He just dug into the trenches and quickly ran the group through the songs. But even after all the complications, he was astonished that they could play this music—note for note—exactly the way they did back in the house. "When Beefheart recorded the *Trout Mask Replica* album, Zappa told me that he was totally amazed at the band because they went into the studio and recorded the entire album . . . in one take—pretty much without stopping," Don Preston recalled. "But the thing was, Zappa wasn't so satisfied with that. . . . Frank said he needed to have the band do a second take just in case he needed to switch things around a bit. So he asked them to do it again, and once again they did the entire album in one take! Zappa was completely amazed because the second takes were virtually identical to the first." During the sessions, Zappa didn't take many suggestions from Kunc for fear that Beefheart would find something else to complain about. In five or six hours, the recording was done, which led many to believe that Zappa just nodded off at the control board. "Dick Kunc was engineering, so he would go, 'Okay,' and we would go . . . and twenty-one tunes later, we were done," Harkleroad said. "Frank was just sitting there.

He didn't really produce the album. There was no musical input, nothing."

Since musical input had only inspired paranoia, Zappa preferred to do his real production work once he got the tapes in his possession. "You couldn't explain, from a technical standpoint, anything to Don," Zappa told Nigel Leigh of the BBC. "You couldn't tell him why things ought to be such and such a way. And it seemed to me that if he was going to create a unique object, the easiest thing for me to do was keep my mouth shut as much as possible." As a rationalist, Zappa was trying to build a foundation for Beefheart's art, while Beefheart, the irrational artist, railed against the perceived limitations Zappa was imposing on him. "I think that if he had been produced by any professional famous producer, there could have been a number of suicides involved," Zappa would later remark. On Easter Sunday 1969, though, Zappa called up Vliet and told him that the album was done. Beefheart had all the guys in the band get dressed up, "as if they were going to Easter church," Zappa recalled. They came over to Zappa's studio early that morning and sat in his living room and listened to it. Apparently, they loved it. Considering all the adversity stirred up in making it, the record's defiant originality cut through the foibles. Within a few months, when a few brave people put the record on their turntable, they would discover just how defiantly original it really was.

Chapter Six
Fast 'N Bulbous

I do not write experimental music. My experimenting is done before I make the music. Afterwards it is the listener who must experiment.

—Edgard Varèse

When *Trout Mask Replica* was released in the US in the early summer of 1969, it was a double LP, not a single CD. It's significant to point this out for a variety of reasons. With an LP, you always had to approach your turntable with it, take out the record from the jacket, and turn it over to play the other side. You had to do this four times with *Trout Mask*. It was like an open dare—a summons—just to see if you could sustain your curiosity long enough to find out what lurked on the other side. With the *Trout Mask* CD, you are left with pretty simple options. For one thing, once you stick the CD in the tray, you never have to touch it until it's over. Secondly, with your remote, you can abruptly skip tracks, or put it on pause while you shake your head in disbelief at what you've just heard. You can quickly turn it off from a safe distance, too, sitting comfortably in your chair. You never ever have to play it again. All things considered, it was far more audacious for *Trout Mask Replica* to come out in the age of the LP. To risk its contents, you constantly had to *handle* it.

Cal Schenkel's cover art for the record merely doubled the dare. With Vliet in his mammoth hat and fish-face, we find the familiar image of the American artist donning a mask to disclose his most impudent work. But the mask doesn't work here, as it does metaphorically in the case of Randy Newman, with subversion hidden under the hood. Beefheart uses the mask as a totem of transformation. He doesn't hide behind it, he becomes the mask. To be a different fish, you first have to *become* the fish. So Cal Schenkel had to find himself one. "The way it came about [was] I went and found this carp head at some fish market," Schenkel explained. "We took it back to my studio, which was the same place that I did the *Uncle Meat* cover . . . and I took this trout head and hollowed it out—the thing stank like hell—and Don had to hold it up to his face for a couple of hours while we shot."

The back cover was less startling, but it didn't make it any easier to approach the music. Mike Barnes, in his Beefheart biography, perfectly described its impact. With the band surrounding him, Beefheart is in his top hat and shades, pointing a shadeless lamp and "looking like a forlorn Mad Hatter, and lighting the way into the wilderness." The inside gatefold design had a color negative photo of the group that was cropped incongruently and shaded by psychedelic colors. However, this was no average psychedelic group. As Barnes would remark, "[T]he Magic Band weren't going to be saddled with any of the beads, bells and incense hokum of the increasingly disparate hippie tribes." Early editions of the record had a lyric sheet featuring a scattering of some of Victor Hayden's lithographs. (These are now included in the CD edition.)

"Frownland" kicks the record off in 7/8 time, until the guitar notes start to fall away aimlessly like raindrops, and French's drums begin to resemble falling rocks. "My smile is stuck," Beefheart declares over the avalanche, "I can't go back to yer frownland." What begins as a basic rock and roll song is quickly swept away with a steel broom. "The standard role of the two guitars, bass, drums rock line-up is subverted to the point where nothing ever settles or is repeated to any extent," Mike Barnes writes in *Captain Beefheart: The Biography*. Beefheart acknowledges his past, where he once built new bridges with blues based material, but the songs featured on *Trout Mask* demand new ears to listen with. "Beefheart is not concerned to build bridges for his audience or to make it any easier for anyone to come along," Langdon Winner reminds us in his "Stranded" essay. "Either you're interested or you're not."

While Beefheart doesn't patronize listeners with this miniature manifesto ("Take my hand 'n come with me / It's not too late for you / It's not too late for me / To find my homeland"), the music arrives with a shocking force that ultimately gives you little choice. "[Beefheart] bellows out a yearning, soulful blues which further warps the already warped structure, pleading, 'I want my own land,' realizing that his wish is becoming fulfilled as he sings the words," Barnes writes. Rock and roll has always been predicated on finding new ways to get the listener onboard, if not up on the dance floor. In "Frownland," Beefheart decries the conventional rules of rock and roll to open up a territory away from standard notation and the precepts of conventional society. "The vision of *Trout Mask Replica* is fundamentally that of an American primitivist surrealist," Langdon Winner explains. "The land he asks us to visit is one we already know very well. It is *not*, as many of us fans have supposed, outer space or the realm of late 1960's hippie, psychedelic weirdness for weirdness' sake." It is America, a self-made country, built on ideas and ideals, both failed and realized, and Beefheart conceives an elaborate map that defines what those attributes mean to him.

The next track, "The Dust Blows Forward 'N the Dust Blows Back," is the first of three a cappella recitations. If "Frownland" points toward a future in a new world, "The Dust Blows Forward" resembles a strange relic unearthed from the distant past. That's partly due to the poem being recorded on a portable cassette machine at the house. The clicking sound of the pause button, which opens the track, is heard repeatedly between each of the vocal passages replicating the clicking heard on old 78s of the needle running through the grooves. But it can also be heard as a picturesque story out of the early American wilderness tales of James Fenimore Cooper, only told through the eyes of a surrealist. The poem begins with ole Gray "with 'er dovewinged hat" and ole Green "with her sewing machine." Exchanging puns for perceptions, the narrator quickly abandons the couple and observes the dust going forward and backward in an endless cycle, while the wind blows black and the industrial smokestacks blow up into the sun's eye. He asks himself if he's gonna die.

The escape from Frownland is also an escape into a wilderness free from ecological calamity and hubris. He's coming back to nature in all its natural folly, where things die only to be born again. In recognition of this, the narrator (who is fishing) is so overwhelmed that he strips off his clothes and feels the breeze blowing through the canyon as well as between his legs. In the end, he's as entranced as Huck Finn was on the riverboat, listening to "mice toes scamperin'," while enjoying his coffee from a "krimpt up can." His girl Bimbo Limbo Spam is happily cradled in his arms as he cheerfully embraces the cycles of the natural world. He's found the peace that Frownland deprived him. By doing the recording on the cassette, Beefheart also leaves the impression that this wondrous world is part of a frontier life quickly becoming a faded memory. "[Beefheart reminds] us of the American myth of the frontiersman and the explorer," writes art critic Roberto Ohrt. "Like the frontiersman, he turns his back on civilization, trusts in his knowledge of nature, and seems at first to be a spinner of unintelligible, wild and fantastic tales." That's the freedom that Beefheart speaks of all through *Trout Mask Replica*, what Walt Whitman had implied when he wrote that "words follow character—nativity, independence, individuality."

In the next song, "Dachau Blues," we're violently thrust back into Frownland, and the air is filled with a different kind of dust and ash. Beefheart's song about the Holocaust jumps out of the mix with an apocalyptic urgency. In intensity, it matches Charley Patton's cry of desperation in "High Water Everywhere" (1929), about the Louisiana flood that ravaged his home state in 1927. The blues became a perfectly appropriate musical form to depict the Dachau death camp, which was the first large-scale concentration camp in southern Germany converted from an old gunpowder factory in 1933. But I have some Jewish friends who feel slightly uncomfortable with Beefheart's abstract rendering of the event. Mike Barnes describes the song quite aptly as "a sonic action painting" and this may be why it causes some unease. Beefheart isn't performing Kaddish here, he's pulling us right into the madness and horror, with images of dancing death skeletons in ovens, confronting us eye-to-eye with "one mad man" while "six million lose."

If "The Dust Blows Forward" describes the natural life cycles, in "Dachau Blues," he decries the cycle of death brought on by war. He dredges up the horror of World War I with "balls 'n powder 'n blood 'n snow," then World War II, where it "rained death 'n showers 'n skeletons." But he's even more concerned about the "sweet children with doves on their shoulders" inheriting the legacy of World War III. As his bass clarinet shrieks over the depicted carnage of the twentieth century, he tells us of these children begging for the end of this misery:

> Countin' out the devil
> With two fingers on their hands
> Beggin' the Lord don't let the third one land
> On World War Three

As the bass clarinet ominously fades on its last note, we suddenly hear an unknown voice on audio cassette telling a story. Is it an old recording of someone who liberated the camps? Is he telling us of what he found there? Not at all. He's talking about rats being beaten out of residences by a bunch of men with sticks, until they finally discovered that their shot-guns worked better. "[T]his was some guy that just showed up at the house," Harkleroad remembered. "[H]e wasn't a friend of anybody's. . . . He came into the house and started telling this story and Don made him stop and repeat it so he could turn on the tape deck."

Zappa had taken Don's own anthropological field record-ing and juxtaposed it with "Dachau Blues" to create a com-parative picture out of two radically different sources. Earlier that year, on *Uncle Meat*, Zappa had taken a recording of drummer Jimmy Carl Black complaining about the poverty of being in the Mothers of Invention. He followed it with a doo-wop song called "The Air." That song had nothing to do with Black's bellyaching, but when you hear the opening lines of "The Air" ("The air / Escaping from your mouth / The hair escaping from your nose"), you immediately connect the two as part of the same story. "The Air" has the effect of answer-ing Black's recorded rant—as does the story of the rats in responding to Beefheart's Holocaust song. It makes a chilling unconscious connection that it was the Nazis who viewed Jews as a form of pestilence.

The tone shifts dramatically with "Ella Guru," a goofy love song that suggests the O'Kaysions' 1968 soul hit "Girl Watcher" on magic mushrooms. "This was a fun tune to play rhythmically, a good upbeat song," Harkleroad remembered. "You throw stuff up in the air and sometimes it falls nicely into place." "Ella Guru" was inspired by a female fan who used to turn up at their live shows in eccentric clothes, incor-porating sheepskin, tie-dye, and ostrich feathers. The song, like her personality, is as light as the air. There are some love-ly verbal puns on her attire ("High yella, high red, high blue, she blew"), plus Jeff Cotton joining into the fray as a leering onlooker possessed of a strangled soprano cartoon voice. The song spawns the infamous sexual in-joke about her being "fast 'n bulbous" (a famous lubricant jelly—credited to Vliet —was also given that designation in Zappa's *Uncle Meat* script). Like some of the libidinous slang in many of the songs on *Uncle Meat*, "fast 'n bulbous" becomes a leitmotif peppered throughout *Trout Mask Replica*.

Continuing in the vein of sexual jargon, the next track, "Hair Pie: Bake 1" ("hair pie" being slang for cunnilingus), is an instrumental recording from the house sessions. "Hair Pie: Bake 1" is a freeform improvised sax duet in the back garden between Beefheart and Victor Hayden. "There were remote mics inside on the instruments and outside on a covered patio next to the laundry shed. This is where Don and Victor stood armed with their respective horns," John French explained. While their sparring resembles some of the wild jazz stylings of Albert Ayler, or perhaps Anthony Braxton, Zappa decided to create an incongruous mix between their duet and the Magic Band simultaneously playing "Hair Pie: Bake 2" in the house. The effect creates a xenochronous composition out of a peculiar matching of quite disparate pieces. It's something he would experiment with on "The Blimp (mousetrapreplica)." Later in his career, Zappa would perform variations on this method on a variety of his own albums. On *Joe's Garage* (1979), for example, he would take guitar solos from various live events and wed them to studio recordings he was doing at the time. In effect, he was paying particular homage to American composer Charles Ives, who many years earlier had laid distinctly different musical pieces on top of one another.

Just as the track builds in intensity, the band abruptly

stops. Two young kids are then heard in the field telling Beefheart that they just came over to hear him play. When they tell him they're from Reseda, Don replies, "She's nice," as if they are describing a friendly neighbour instead of a town. After an uneasy silence, Don asks, "Whaddya think?" "Sounds good," they answer as if not really sure what constituted "good." "It's a bush recording," Don intones confidently. "We're out recording with bush," thus unwittingly linking cunnilingus ("hair pie") with "bush," which is slang for pubic hair. In a moment of confusion, Don tells the kids that the composition is called "Neon Meate Dream of a Octafish." They nod affirmatively as if no title would make sense of what they just experienced. As he lights a cigarette, Don suddenly realizes it is "Hair Pie."

John Corbett, in the essay "The Dust Blows Back" included in the comprehensive CD box set *Grow Fins: Captain Beefheart & His Magic Band: Rarities [1965–1982]*, suggests that the "bush" recording (featuring the sounds of some fauna shaking thus making the point) is "reminiscent of Peter Brotzmann and Han Bennink's *Schwarzwaldfahrt*, a trip for the two Middle European free improvisers into the Black Forest to make a racket on the trees, in the streams, with the birds, accompanied only by a Stellavox tape recorder." When we hear Don mention "Neon Meate Dream of a Octafish" to the kids in the field recording, it anticipates a song we don't actually hear until later on the record. Frank Zappa, on *Freak Out!*, did something similar when he included a clip from "Help, I'm a Rock" in the middle bridge of the earlier "Who Are the Brain Police?" In both cases, Beefheart and Zappa play with the very concept of linear time on a record. Mike Barnes, in his Beefheart biography, tells us that the two kids who happened on to the field with Beefheart were actually friends of Eric Drew Feldman (who would later join the Magic Band in 1976).

Once the powerhouse performance of "Moonlight on Vermont" concludes side one, the second side opens with a proclamation: "A squid eating dough in a polyethylene bag is fast 'n bulbous. Got me?" In the case of Beefheart and Zappa, the idea of couching sexual innuendo in their songs came out of the blues and R&B records they listened to as kids. Many doo-wop bands like the Clovers were famous for this, as were rockers like Little Richard. Even the sly Fats Domino couldn't resist insinuating what thrill he found on Blueberry Hill. Out of the gag, "Pachuco Cadaver" quickly jumps in with a rather melodious boogie shuffle. "It was another one that was fun to play because again we're all playing in a similar time and key—the guitar parts and drums are in sync," Bill Harkleroad told Billy James. But the tune instantly shifts out of gear once Beefheart steps forward. "When she wears her bolero then she begin t' dance / All the pachucos start withholdin' hands," he sings. The term Pachuco is an LA term for the young adolescent Mexican-Americans in the 40s and 50s who wore stylish Zoot suits, and the song is a surreal love lyric to their lifestyle.

Although the title "Pachuco Cadaver" suggests something morbid, it's actually a richly textured love song ("She wears her past like a present," Beefheart says admiringly with a twinkle in his pun). Beefheart doesn't so much sing this tune as he does recite it, filling the song with stream-of-consciousness phrases. "Beefheart's vocals . . . rely less upon the melody of any given tune than upon the music present in the way people actually talk," Langdon Winner explains. "Thus, the singing—

and it is definitely singing—on 'Pachuco Cadaver' takes the form of the rising and falling emphatic tones of an Old West storyteller." While name-checking Kathleen Winsor's period novel *Forever Amber*, which was once considered controversial for its sexual explicitness, Beefheart incorporates it as a pun for the amber brody knob spinner. This term was slang for the turn knob on the handlebars of 50s Chevys used to pick up girls (these same brody knobs are referred to by Zappa, too, on "The Uncle Meat Variations," where he dips into the pool of 50s pop culture lore). As the song winds down, Beefheart plays a hearty sax solo over the vamp.

Speaking of cadavers, the next song, "Bill's Corpse," is about one. Bill Harkleroad has always assumed that the song was written for him. But it's more likely about Beefheart's dead pet goldfish, Bill, in keeping with the fish motif of the album. According to Mike Barnes, Beefheart had overfed Bill, ultimately leading to his demise. The song uses Bill's death as a starting point for one of many observations on the comparative life cycles between humans and the world of nature. "The only way they ever all got together," Beefheart declares, "was not in love but shameful grief." But these aren't the thoughts he wants to treasure. Whether he's singing about love, sex, or death, Beefheart connects everything to mortality and its huge role played in nature's hierarchy. "Sweet Sweet Bulbs" is a love song to the garden that Beefheart cultivated at the house, connecting his love for its blooming splendour with his own sexual passion for a woman. "She walked back into nature uh queen uncrowned," he sings. "She had just recognized herself to be an heir t' the throne."

On "Neon Meate Dream of a Octafish," he shifts into a scene of wild wet sex unfolding passionately. The subject of the song, in fact, becomes inseparable from the frenzy of poetic verse that Beefheart unravels:

> neon meate dream of a octafish
> artificial rose petals
> in flesh petals and pots
> in fact in feast
> in tubes
> tubs
> bulbs
> in jest incest injust in feast incest
> in specks
> in speckled spreckled
> speckled
> speculation

As part of his transformation into a different fish, the very trout mask of the cover art, he transforms his own being into a living language that takes pleasure in its own sensual sound. Sex and language in this song become intertwined. "Van Vliet alludes to the Imagist concept of being very precise in descriptions, and the Surrealist concept of juxtaposing opposites to generate new forms," Mike Barnes writes. "The song is a journey through a luxuriant forest of language which Van Vliet recites in pinched, breathless tones, onomatopoeically evoking the slippery wetness of sex."

When Talking Heads recorded Hugo Ball's 1916 Dadaist sound poem "I Zimbra" for their 1979 *Fear of Music* album, they simply created a facsimile of the verse, presenting it as a monotonous sing-along chorus in a bed of dance-pop African rhythms. In "Neon Meate Dream of a Octafish"

Beefheart doesn't appropriate Ball, as the Talking Heads do, he creates his very own incantation in the spirit of Ball. The sensuality in Beefheart's Dadaist free-association, like Ball, gets drawn from the sound of the words themselves. In Beefheart's case, they take on as densely a musical texture as the music supporting him. The lyrics are, as Zappologist Sean Bonney accurately describes in his essay, "*Trout Mask Replica: A Dagger in the Head of Mojo Man,*" words "[that] are experienced as material entities that themselves change into one another, just as plants grow from their bulbs in the song, and transform into fists and flesh and body fluids." Unlike traditional love songs that feature suitors seeking partners in life and in bed, Beefheart goes inside the giddy sensations of mating. "His songs were commonly characterised by a determined avoidance of cliches in both the musical structure and lyrical content—instead of bragging about his prowess as a lover and his ability to conquer sexually, Beefheart's words would become lost in the frenzy and enjoyment of a sexual encounter," Graham Johnston writes in his essay, "Clicks and Klangs: Gender and the Avant-Garde." In expressing that frenzy, Beefheart plays the simran horn, creating the hollow ambience of an air tunnel. Later, Beefheart solos on a miniature bagpipe called a musette, which Bonney describes as sounding like "the offspring of a half-asphyxiated Hammond organ with a North African pan pipe."

Where "Neon Meate Dream of a Octafish" plunges into an erotic soundscape of the future, "China Pig" revisits the past. It might even be a throwback to earlier Beefheart. "China Pig" is a standard blues arrangement recorded on the cassette machine during the house sessions. In the spirit of the past, it features the return of the prodigal son, Doug

Moon, on guitar. "'China Pig' came about just totally off the cuff," Harkleroad recalled. "[Doug Moon] came down for a visit and was playing this straightahead blues thing and Don really reacted to it in a positive way—almost turning around to us and saying, 'Well, why don't you guys play this way?' We felt like saying, 'Well we used to, but it's hard to remember how, since it's been nine months of twelve-hour days trying to do these other things.'" The irony of Doug Moon's participation on *Trout Mask*, after being dismissed for not being adventurous enough, wasn't lost on many present that day. The song begins as a run-through of Mississippi John Hurt's "Candy Man," but it quickly evolves into a blues song about the singer's ambivalence toward breaking his porcelain piggy bank.

"Do one of those u-chunk-u-chunk, slow one . . . ," Don urges Moon, who begins launching into a slow blues in A7. Just as he did in the days of Studio Z with Zappa, Beefheart performed "China Pig" in one room while Moon dutifully picked out the chords in another. The sound they create is pretty much bootleg quality, containing some of the atmosphere of an old Charley Patton record. If it wasn't for the brief speeding up of the cassette tape toward the end, caused when someone attempted to shut off the recording prematurely, this might have been a song unearthed from the 30s. By leaving the tape glitch in, however, Beefheart and Zappa deliberately make us conscious of the recording process as part of the actual song.

"My Human Gets Me Blues" is a nice piece of rock be-bop about sexual confusion that demonstrates just how dexterous the group had become in their marathon rehearsals. "That was a song that all of us were pretty excited about," Harkleroad eagerly remarked. "It unified the band more than a lot of other tunes." Beefheart's reading is so assured that you can hear his delight in breaking down the English language into delicious morsels of vowels and consonants ("With yer jaw hangin' slack 'n yer hair's curlin' / Like an ole navy fork stickin' in the sunset"). "[Beefheart] refused to use civilized English in a linear, logical way and learned the entire language as a vast and amusing game," Langdon Winner writes. "A barrage of puns, rhymes, illogicalities, absurd definitions, and unending word play fills the dialogue with a wonderful confusion."

"Dali's Car" is a complex instrumental ballad, the first song composed explicitly for *Trout Mask*. It was inspired by a visit the group took to a Salvador Dalí exhibit at the LA County Art Museum during their early rehearsals. Composed by candlelight, when the power had gone out in the street, it was a pivotal song for John French, who couldn't relinquish Dalí's pervasive imagery. "This [visit] changed my concept of the drums," French recalled. "I was impressed not only with Dalí's photographic technique, but with his ability to superimpose images within other images, as though seeing in more than three dimensions." What makes "Dali's Car" so distinct is that it has dimensions built into its guitar chords. Once French taught it to the group, it became a compellingly discordant lullaby. "'Dali's Car' was a duet with Jeff [Cotton] and myself," Harkleroad explained. "It was this dissonant thing that was rhythmically very tight . . . we could play it in our sleep all night long exactly like that everytime!"

"Hair Pie: Bake 2" is the studio version (minus Beefheart and Hayden's horn duet from the house session) of the original song. Once again, the instrumental track perfectly confounds our expectations, or perhaps, our desire for a rhythmic sequence that harmonizes. Instead, as Langdon Winner would point out, Beefheart "delights in jamming these expectations. His songs begin a rhythmic pattern, let it run for a couple of measures, and then break it off only to strike up something completely different." In "Hair Pie: Bake 2, according to Winner, there are no fewer than fourteen separate beats and melodies that are quickly introduced, briefly played, and then abruptly dropped.

As "Hair Pie: Bake 2" hastily concludes, some laughter from Beefheart erupts. Once more, we are thrust into a burlesque routine involving Beefheart's love of the phrase "fast 'n bulbous." As Zappa conducts, Victor Hayden and Beefheart trade quips as if spontaneously constructing a poem. Hayden happily shouts the phrase, "fast 'n bulbous!" After which, Beefheart jumps in with, "That's right, the Mascara Snake, fast 'n bulbous!" lewdly caressing the word "bulbous." To which Hayden replies proudly, "Bulbous also tapered." Too quick, apparently, for Beefheart, and missing a line. He states impatiently, "You're supposed to wait until I say, 'Also, a tin teardrop.'" Hayden either can't believe what he's doing here, or he's surprised that he simply forgot the line. "Oh . . . Christ," he mutters disbelievingly. "Again, beginning!" conductor Zappa cries as if the string section momentarily fucked up a crucial bar of music. The second time through, though, they get it. Spot on. On the beat. "That's right," Beefheart says approvingly.

Some may see the routine as more of Zappa's juvenile preoccupations, without recognizing that (like Beefheart) he enjoyed interpreting human speech in musical terms. While both men explored that phenomenon in different ways, Zappa often cut disparate pieces of dialogue and music together to create texture and tempo in a musical composition —heard particularily on *Lumpy Gravy*. With *Uncle Meat*, and especially *Weasels Ripped My Flesh*, Zappa created one huge collage out of a series of disparate songs and recitations. In conceptual terms, Zappa similarily shaped *Trout Mask* as a way to continually contrast the atonal textures in Beefheart's music. "Dissonance when it's unresolved is like having a headache," Zappa once explained to journalist Bob Marshall. "So, the most interesting music, as far as I'm concerned, is music in which dissonance is created, sustained for the proper amount of time, and resolved."

When the song "Pena" follows the blithe silliness of the "fast 'n bulbous" interlude, Zappa's process of resolving dissonance gets reversed. "Pena" may be the harshest tune on the record. One reason for that is that it's sung by Mark Boston, in his hysterically shrieking soprano voice. The other reason may be the unsettling nature of the song itself. The singer witnesses a girl sitting herself upon a burning waffle iron while sunning herself. The accident causes him to vomit "beautifully," whereby he provides a band-aid to her burned area. Growing tired and sore from sitting, she promptly gets up and stubs her toe. While recovering, she lets a yellow butterfly out of a blue felt box. The insect resembles in size and shape the white pulps in her sores. The stark delirium of Cotton's voice disclosing this surreal event creates an unbearable tension that you can't escape from.

"Well" is an abstract existential poem that's told as a traditional blues holler. The blues holler was discovered in the Southern Delta of the early part of the twentieth century, where itinerant black muleskinners worked in the levee. While feeling the pangs of homesickness, they conversely felt the joys of freely roaming from job to job. Even if they worked under the lousiest conditions, under the worst boss, they would act out their anger by singing humorous and racy tall tales. This musical form would eventually be extended to chain gang workers in the penitentiary. Alan Lomax, along with his father, John A. Lomax, did many field recordings of these blues hollers. He describes their distinctive musical rhythms in a manner that might have appealed to Beefheart. "They are solos, slow in tempo, free in rhythm . . . composed of long, gliding, ornamented, and melismatic phrases, given a melancholy character by minor intervals as well as by blued or bent tones," Lomax explains. Those long, gliding melismatic phrases, free in rhythm, are exactly what Beefheart achieves in "Well":

> My mind cracked like custard
> Ran red until it sealed
> Turn t' wooden 'n rolled like uh wheel well well

Unlike "China Pig," which invoked the ambience of an old 78 recording, "Well" is an a cappella recording done in the studio with a modernist sound. Beefheart's booming Ahab voice, enhanced by added reverb, rails against the echoes of his own defiant chants.

"When Big Joan Sets Up" is a fiercely energetic track about a large woman who can't go outside for fear of being humiliated by others. This stunningly intricate hybrid of blues and free jazz bursts into a colorfully expressionistic portrait of sexual disorientation. Beefheart's voice continually shifts dramatically in the song from pure swing into rhythmless pockets featuring his wildly frenetic sax stylings. "His voice never merely interprets a tune," Roberto Ohrt rightly points out. "It gives reality to the most important part of his music, one that is impossible to record in music notation." "When Big Joan Sets Up" is the closest Beefheart comes on *Trout Mask* in approximating the influence painting has had on his musical compositions.

After another comic routine, where Mark Boston as Rockette Morton informs us that he runs "on beans—laser beans," the song "Fallin' Ditch" follows. It is Beefheart's answer to Blind Lemon Jefferson's 1927 "See That My Grave Is Kept Clean." Jefferson was an East Texas blues singer, born in 1897, with a reed-thin voice and a stunning virtuoso guitar style. Beefheart often covered Jefferson's ominous "Black Snake Moan," but "Fallin' Ditch" is his tribute to Jefferson's startling defiance of Death. Like Jefferson, he offers Death a nimble taunt:

> Who's afraid of the spirit with the bluesferbones
> Who's afraid of the fallin' ditch
> Fallin' ditch ain't gonna get my bones

Beefheart's voice is loud and truculent, riding on the acceleration of John French's percussion, wildly jerking against the guitar lines that pull at him like thick ropes dragging him into the ground.

"Sugar 'N Spikes," like "Moonlight on Vermont," was demoed before Bill Harkleroad joined the band. "[T]he parts were really stretching out from the blues," Harkleroad explained. "It was like a blues band only with an orchestrated classical feel to it." Part of that classical feel comes right out of one of the melodic lines that Mike Barnes credits to Miles

Davis's "Concierto de Aranjuez," heard on *Sketches of Spain* (1960). Among their diet of blues and R&B, Zappa and Beefheart also listened intently to this album. "Ant Man Bee," a funky track about the ambiguous relationship between man and nature, has one of the simplest arrangements on the record. "The beat on 'Ant Man Bee' was just him sitting down one day [at the drums]," John French recalled. "On *Trout Mask*, where at a later point we didn't have time for me to write down all the drum parts, he just sat down and played an idea of what he wanted." Bill Harkleroad heard something closer to the pan-African sound he discovered later on John Coltrane records. "I'd listened to Coltrane's *Africa/Brass* but just never, ever got that feeling," Harkleroad explained. "John French put that African feel across because of the way he played drums. . . . He was really ahead of his time." Captain Beefheart summed up the song's meaning to Langdon Winner, "If you give [the ants] sugar, they won't have to eat the poison."

During the sessions for *Uncle Meat*, Frank Zappa recorded a lovely honky-tonk instrumental version of a traditional sea chanty called "Handsome Cabin Boy." "[It's] a song about the bogus certification of sailors," Zappa explained. "A girl goes on a boat dressed as a boy and gets pregnant. The lyrics are all about who done it." Zappa had heard the song on the record *Blow Boys Blow*, a collection of rowdy and profane sea ballads, interpreted by Ewan MacColl and A. L. Lloyd. The collaboration of these two folk legends, in the early sixties, was an attempt to, as they put it in the album's liner notes, create the fidelity of the original songs while bringing deeper shadings to the dramatic material within them. "The stereotype of the roaring brutal sea-dog is present in nearly all the songs in this album, but the careful listener will perceive, beyond the toughness and the irony, a deep unease, an ache, a longing for something better," they wrote. After listening repeatedly to the record, he loaned it to Beefheart. Or, at least, that's how the story goes. "He gave it to me!" Beefheart railed in protest, still miffed years later in 1994. Whatever the truth, the song "Orange Claw Hammer," which opens the final side of *Trout Mask Replica*, has both the toughness and the ache that Lloyd and MacColl sought on their album.

The recitation, which took two hours to record on the cassette machine, is the most sustained and satisfying dramatic reading on the record. There is an unyielding tension here, as if we're hearing a song in the process of creating itself. Bob Dylan once accomplished this feat on "I'm Not There," an unreleased song featured on a bootleg collection of his complete 1967 basement tapes with the Band. Dylan's track, a love song about failed commitment, has him singing lyrics that seem to be invented on the spot. The effect doesn't so much complete his thoughts as it reveals something about how language begins to define itself as thought. On "Orange Claw Hammer," Beefheart tells his own story of failed commitment, of familial despair, where the singer appears to be seeking words that his feelings have yet to register. A father, who has been living at sea, finally confronts his long-lost daughter years later. But the tale is told through a spree of quick pulsating images that unnerve the singer as the story unfolds. In this illusively told tale, powerfully provocative images continuously stab into the mortal fears of this peg-legged sailor:

> Uh beautiful sagebrush jack rabbit
> 'n an oriole sang like an orange

His breast full uh worms
'n his tail clawed the evenin' like uh hammer

Once again, with the clicking of the tape recorder's pause button punctuating each line, Beefheart lets the story tell itself
rather than trying to impose a narrative onto it. "The song
works not for what it says to us but for the way it joggles out
an inherited store of fantasies about drifters, seaports, pirates,
and the separation of fathers and children," Langdon Winner
writes in "Stranded." "Orange Claw Hammer" evokes the
pathos in the painful reunion of father and daughter without
pulling heartstrings to achieve it. In 1976, while on tour with
Zappa's band, he and Beefheart sat in a radio station and performed a plaintive version of "Orange Claw Hammer."
Beefheart confidently sang the song, rather than letting it sing
him. Meanwhile, Zappa's acoustic guitar, which accompanied
Beefheart's performance, always kept the narrative hurtling
forward (the way Ralph Rinzler's and Steve Benbow's guitars
do on the songs featured on *Blow Boys Blow*). In this rare happy
moment between them, Zappa provided a cozy bed for
Beefheart's unrequited longing.

   "People are just too far out—far away from nature,"
Beefheart said in *Rolling Stone*. "Wild Life" tells us just how far.
It's the perhaps the most prescient of Beefheart's songs on
Trout Mask Replica, since he would eventually abandon the
music business and retreat to a trailer far removed from urban
centres altogether. "Wild Life," though, is hardly the most
lyrically imaginative track ("Wild life along with my wife / I'm
goin' up on the mountain fo' the rest uh m' life"), but outside
of "When Big Joan Sets Up" and the conclusion of "Ant Man
Bee," it does have some of Beefheart's finest horn solos. On

"Wild Life," he even tries to imitate his own speech patterns. "[I]t was the best horn playing Don did," Harkleroad asserted. "Of course, he didn't know what he was doing, but he got pretty good at squeezing out a great tone." It was such a good tone that in 1982, Magic Band guitarist Gary Lucas transcribed the sax solo for his guitar melody on "The Host the Ghost Most Holy-O" included on *Ice Cream for Crow*.

"She's Too Much for My Mirror" is a sparklingly funny little number about romantic ambivalence:

> She's too much for my mirror
> She almost makes me lose it
> The way she abuse it
> Make me never want to use it

It opens casually with an intro by engineer Dick Kunc that once more makes us conscious of the act of listening to a record in production, in short, making us participants in the process. "Here you would have a famous version of 'She's Too Much for My Mirror.' Note the clever slate," Kunc says cheerfully, while marking the take with his clapper. "'She's Too Much for My, or Anybody's, Mirror', number two. Told ya." On his own records, Zappa would often thrust Kunc into the mix, once again to provide texture, or maybe to render contrast between the previous song and the one to follow. He did this to great effect, for example, at the beginning of "Idiot Bastard Son" on *We're Only in It for the Money*. "This will be a little vocal TH-Heaven right here on Earth," Kunc called out mockingly in a killer parody of an AM radio jock setting up a song.

"She's Too Much for My Mirror" is a runaway track that

almost runs away with itself. Since Beefheart didn't attend rehearsals, it was often miraculous that he could fit his lyrics into any of the music created by the band. In this instance, it almost didn't happen. "Don sounds uptight when he's singing it," Harkleroad recalled. "This is something that could have been fixed if he had actually sung at rehearsals." Beefheart can be heard at the conclusion saying, "Shit, I don't know how I'm gonna get that in there." Apparently, he still had a page of lyrics that never found their way into the song's quick tempo.

If there was one song rehearsed relentlessly in the house sessions, with guitar lines continuously being sung and discussed, it was "Hobo Chang Ba." Essentially, it's a folk song about Chinese immigrants coming to America and building the railroads, and one (Chang Ba) who becomes a hobo. Beefheart sings in a low monotonous drawl that mirrors the dreariness suffered by Chang Ba:

> The rails I ride 'r rustin
> The new sunrise I'm trustin'
> Strawwood claw rattlin' m' jaw

For Bizarre/Straight Records, however, "Hobo Chang Ba" inspired a whole different kind of dreariness. Herb Cohen noticed that Beefheart had ordered twenty sets of sleigh bells for the recording session. He pointed out to Beefheart that even if Frank Zappa and the engineer were added to the bell-ringers, they would only need fourteen sleigh bells with one in each hand of the performers. "What are you going to do with the other six?," Cohen asked. "We'll overdub them," Beefheart replied calmly.

If *Trout Mask Replica* overall is an attempt to make the disparate parts of a group work together musically, "The Blimp (mousetrapreplica)" goes one step further by adding another group to the mix: the Mothers of Invention. Zappa was working in the Whitney studio mixing a freeform jazz parody from the Mothers' last tour fittingly called "Charles Ives," a tune that had been played quite frequently on the tour. Sometimes it was part of another song, "Didja Get Any Onya?" an atonal horn workout that also featured comic burlesque, operatic falsettos, and a brief trumpet quote from Ives's *The Unanswered Question*. Midway through the mixing session, Zappa received a phone call in the studio from Beefheart, who was excited about some new lyrics. Beefheart had Jeff Cotton recite them over the phone, to the accompaniment of Beefheart's soprano sax, and Zappa decided to record it. He superimposed the recording (in the style of Charles Ives) over the Mothers' song he was working on. "You can tell it's not us—just listen to the studio quality of the recording of those parts compared to the things we did," Harkleroad pointed out. "Maybe we didn't have that studio polish, but then again we weren't about studio polish, cardboard drums and tortured guitars were more us." It was a key observation because the final results are fascinating for what they reveal.

Hard at work, Zappa begins the track by asking Cotton, over the phone, if he's ready. Once Zappa tells him to begin, Cotton delivers a frenzied account of sexual terror:

> The drazy hoops the drazy hoops
> They're camp they're camp
> Tit tits the blimp the blimp

The frantic words juxtapose perfectly with the Mothers' smoothly crafted abstract jazz performance. The wedding of these two contrasting pieces also paints a fascinating portrait of Beefheart and Zappa's dissimilar styles. On the one hand, you can hear in "The Blimp (mousetrapreplica)," Zappa's conscious desire to prove that one size fits all. For him, this is a calculated strategy, one he's been consciously designing and mapping out through his entire musical career. On the other hand, Beefheart's strategy is more intuitive, playfully haphazard, part of what writer Neil Slaven calls "a living environment." Steve Peacock explores these differences with keen insight in *Sounds* magazine:

> Zappa is a fine technician, a craftsman with a wealth of expert knowledge on which he draws to construct intricate . . . (though bizarre) set pieces of music. He blends absurdity, outrage with an extensive, wide-ranging set of musical reference points. Listening to Zappa's music is a thoroughly enjoyable experience and though there is an emotive quality, the overriding effect is intellectual. . . . Frank Zappa constructs and controls his music, it is for the most part conscious creation; Captain Beefheart opens up and lets it flow. Frank Zappa is shrewd, Beefheart is a visionary.

The two incongruent musical pieces illustrate perfectly the shrewdly organized chaos of the Mothers versus the spontaneous hyperbole at the core of Beefheart's visionary art. "The Blimp (moustrapreplica)" is a marvellous blending of two disperate sensibilities, as (in a completely different musical sense) "We Can Work it Out" was for Lennon and McCartney. Both songs, in their own very distinct ways, succeed in transforming incongruency into a new style of harmony.

"Steal Softly Thru Snow" may be the most romantically sublime track on the album. "Grain grows rainbows up straw hill," Beefheart sings wistfully. "Breaks my heart to see the highway 'cross the hills / Man lived a million years 'n still kills." As romantic as the sentiment is, the song's construction is a killer. "The drum parts on ['Steal Softly' and 'Hair Pie'] were figured out partially during rehearsal and partially by me writing it out later," French explained. "I wrote a lot of my own drum parts for the album. And what I did was take the music and take the main rhythmic thrust of each instrument and try and combine it into one part." Apparently, French had to combine some awkward musical phrases. "Some people were playing [in] five, some people were playing [in seven], some were playing [in] three, some in four," French said. "Now I knew that I wasn't going to play in three different time signatures at the same time on all these songs, but what I wanted to do was grab the essence of what the part was and make a part that would suggest tying them together—even though it was going to be a counter rhythm, just like everything else." Naturally, it was agony for the group to learn. "I remember torturing myself to play the thing," Harkleroad explained remembering the torture. Yet he still considered it his favorite song on the record. "This is the tune that has the most to offer. The unison rhythm things and John French's playing on it is ripping!" Harkleroad enthused.

In "Old Fart at Play," the trout mask is finally unveiled. The verse, an excerpt from an unfinished novel, is Beefheart's final transformation into a different fish. "As [the old fart] looks on, a metamorphosis begins to take place in him,"

Langdon Winner explains. "The mask grows more and more fishlike. The boundaries between man, artifact, and natural creature quickly vanish." This transformation into a state of natural being erodes boundaries and openly gives into change. The song explicitly states the quest of the album: it's about breathing in the freedom of your true nature, to discover yourself "breathin' freely," as the Old Fart puts it. The Beefheart trout mask is a disguise that reveals, rather than hides. "His excited eyes from within the dark interior glazed, watered in appreciation of his thoughtful preparation," he recites at the end. He has finally jumped out of school, to a place where freedom is experienced rather than consciously defined. Although "Veteran's Day Poppy" literally concludes *Trout Mask Replica*, it's "Old Fart at Play" that provides the more natural conclusion.

Beefheart's desire to be different on *Trout Mask Replica* wasn't designed to oppose anybody, or anything. "Van Vliet's version of freedom is the mastery of a man who cannot make anyone else's music," Greil Marcus writes in *Ranters & Crowd Pleasers: Pop in Punk Music, 1977–92*. "As he has proved in the past, a man who can't make anyone else's music is not the same as a man who won't." But Beefheart came to see that freedom can impose its own limitations. In the years following the release of *Trout Mask Replica*, many would come to both scorn and love this record, while others would be ready to jump into the pond Beefheart created for them. Beefheart, though, in short time would begin to feel like a fish out of water.

Epilogue
Everybody Drinks
from the Same Pond

Let me recite what history teaches. History teaches.
—Gertrude Stein

To understand the shock and disbelief surrounding the release of *Trout Mask Replica*, in the early summer of 1969, you first had to consider the music already on the airwaves, or perhaps about to arrive there. The previous year, politically and culturally, had been relentlessly convulsive. America was still reeling in shock from a succession of horrors. Martin Luther King was shot dead and cities were in flames. Robert Kennedy, the great hope of the Democratic Party, was murdered like his brother five years earlier. Richard Nixon would inherit the crown of the Presidency, bringing with him a dark cloud that began to cover the country. The Soviet army put the boot to Czechoslovakia's "socialism with a human face" during the short-lived Prague Spring. The war in Vietnam was continuously escalating. After the violence at the Democratic

Convention in Chicago, radical politics was beginning to turn criminally psychopathic with the Weather Underground, while counterculture living was becoming cultish. Charles Manson and his murderous hippie family were merely a year away—acting out their horrors a mere month after the release of *Trout Mask*.

In the aftermath of 1968, you could feel the culture starting to splinter into factions. You could also hear it in the music—still vital, but seeking shelter from the storm. The aching harmonies of country rock were just being fully realized when Gram Parsons and Chris Hillman of the Byrds formed the Flying Burrito Brothers with their first record, *The Gilded Palace of Sin*. Another Byrd, David Crosby, plus former Buffalo Springfield singer/songwriter Steven Stills and ex-Hollie Graham Nash, brought their own gentle angst to the creation of Crosby, Stills & Nash. British chanteuse Dusty Springfield turned up in Memphis to prove that she was perhaps the best white soul singer of her time. Elvis Presley rediscovered his own soul making a confidently crafted studio record, *From Elvis in Memphis*, shortly after a surprisingly successful television special. The Beatles, meanwhile, were about to acrimoniously depart the stage they erected with the late summer release of *Abbey Road*. After being upstaged by Jimi Hendrix at Monterey, the Who decided to throw down the gauntlet and create the first epic rock opera about a blind, sagelike pinball wizard named Tommy. A ten-year-old singer from Gary, Indiana, named Michael Jackson was on a mission to change black R&B along with his brothers, the Jackson 5. Led Zeppelin was born out of the ashes of the Yardbirds to unleash what came to be known as heavy metal.

Into this eclectic gumbo of pop metamorphosis, with the

birth of Woodstock Nation in the wings and its violent death a mere few months later at Altamont, *Trout Mask Replica* appeared on the scene totally oblivious to the musical, political, and cultural environment surrounding it. The other performers that summer, who were making their shift toward either stardom or oblivion, made their moves with one eye on the pop audience they carried on their backs. Captain Beefheart & the Magic Band made no concessions to anyone. They came out of a hermitage, not a popular culture. They emerged from a house, and they did it with music that nobody expected to hear. For those who did hear it, the record would polarize an already polarized culture. It repelled some just as violently as it attracted listeners. "When I first heard *Trout Mask Replica*, I about puked," *Rolling Stone* critic Ed Ward put it, not so delicately. "What *is* this shit, I thought. People I met talked about it in glowing terms—not just anybody, mind you, but people I genuinely respected when it came to their music tastes." One of those people he respected was an ambitious and talented writer named Lester Bangs. Bangs wrote about *Trout Mask Replica* as if the Messiah had just arrived to heal a broken nation. "Captain Beefheart, the only true dadaist in rock, has been victimized repeatedly by public incomprehension and critical authoritarianism," Bangs told *Rolling Stone* readers. "[His] music [derives] as much from the new free jazz and African chant rhythms as from Delta blues, the songs tended to be rattly and wayward, clattering along on weirdly jabbering high-pitched guitars and sprung rhythms."

Eliot Wald, writing a few years later in *Oui*, knew what Bangs had heard in *Trout Mask*, but he also understood what offended listeners as well. "[Lester Bangs] described [*Trout Mask*] as the most astounding and important work of art ever to appear on a phonograph record," he began. "However, it was not to everyone's taste. . . . Rhythms are totally unpredictable; what starts out as a blues boogie may end up sounding like a surrealist waltz. Everybody seems to be playing whatever came to mind, including Beefheart, whose sax, musette and simran horn solos (played through tubes that allow him to play two instruments at the same time) swoop and dive, mirroring his incredible four-octave voice. Lyrically, it's absurdist poetry. . . . *Trout Mask Replica* was not an overnight sensation." Not only was it not an overnight sensation, it took (for some people) many nights of listening to fully comprehend its strange power. "The first time I heard *Trout Mask*, when I was fifteen years old, I thought it was the worst thing I'd ever heard," remembered Matt Groening, the creator of *The Simpsons*, and long-time fan and friend of Frank Zappa. "I said to myself, 'They're not even trying!' It was just a sloppy cacophony. Then I listened to it a couple more times because I couldn't believe Frank Zappa could do this to me— and because a double album cost a lot of money. About the third time, I realized they were doing it on purpose: they meant it to sound exactly this way. About the sixth or seventh time, it clicked in and I thought it was the greatest album I ever heard."

The greatest album ever heard? In 1987, *Rolling Stone* did list it as number 33 in their Top 100 Best Rock Albums issue, describing it as "rock's most visionary album." Critic Paul Gambaccini later gathered other scribes who listed the record at number 81 in a Top 100 list of the best rock and roll albums of all time. *The Illustrated Encyclopedia of Rock* describes *Trout Mask* as "one of the most advanced overall concepts in rock music." *Record Collector* describes Beefheart's epic opus as "a major musical achievement," while the *Trouser Press Record Guide* calls it a "masterpiece." As recent as March 2005, *Mojo* magazine declared *Trout Mask* the "ultimate Out There! album." It was a "triumph of genius" (beating out such competition as Sun Ra's 1973 *Space Is the Place*, on which his Astro Intergalactic Infinity Arkestra attempted to musically define the history of the universe) according to the popular British music magazine and "matched by a collective work ethic that threatened the health of everyone involved." British music critic Ben Watson couldn't compare *Trout Mask* to any other recording. "*Trout Mask* is the only record ever made for which no other music is suitable 'preparation,'" he wrote.

As visionary as *Trout Mask* is, its influence in the years to follow was not as straightforward as other significant pop artists. As critic Steve Huey remarked, "[T]he influence of *Trout Mask Replica* was felt more in spirit than in direct copycatting, as a catalyst rather than a literal musical starting point." That spirit, which stretched itself down many winding pathways, proved Beefheart right when he pronounced one day that everyone drinks from the same pond. One such drinker from that pond was John Graham Mellor, a middleclass grave digger, who would later be reborn as Joe Strummer. Years before he dreamed of making a dent in the rock conglomerate with the Clash, Strummer told critic Greil Marcus, "When I was sixteen, [*Trout Mask Replica*] was the only record I listened to—for a year." Marcus actually heard *Trout Mask* stewing under the surface of the Clash's 1977 debut. "The Clash have taken Beefheart's aesthetic of scorched vocals, guitar discords, melody reversals, and rhythmic conflict and made the whole seem anything but avantgarde: in their hands that aesthetic speaks with clarity and immediacy, a demand you have to accept or refuse," he wrote in *New West* in 1978. That either/or ultimatum, which became the standard provocation offered by punk in the late 70s, wasn't exactly the stand that *Trout Mask* took when it appeared in 1969. Beefheart held a more an ambiguous position than punk itself offered. *Trout Mask Replica* was an inhabitor of the pond, possessing those who wished to be different fish.

Another artist transformed was Mark Mothersbaugh, the founder of the synth-punk band Devo. Formed in Akron, Ohio, in 1972, by two Kent State art students, Mothersbaugh and Jerry Casale came upon the notion of a "devolving" American society out of the ashes of the fatal shootings of four students at Kent State by the National Guard. In their mind, mankind was regressing, becoming rigid in its thinking and more authoritarian in attitude. Devo mirrored that world in their music with robotic rhythms and nerdish demeanour. "Beefheart was a major influence on Devo as far as direction goes," Mothersbaugh explained in 1978. "*Trout Mask Replica* . . . there's so many people that were affected by that album that he probably doesn't even know about, a silent movement of people." That movement of people seemed silent only because the record, nurtured in isolation, inspired a quiet need to be unique. So its spirit became shared subliminally among a scattering of diverse voices in a wilderness.

One such individual was Lora Logic (Sara Whitby), formerly of the punk band X-Ray Spex, who found the post-punk ensemble Essential Logic in 1978. In her song, "Aerosol Burns," from *Fanfare in the Garden*, her voice bursts forth like Bjork on steroids as she breaks the song's title into spit consonants and vowels. While twisting her saxophone into squeaks curling around the broken sounds, Logic marries some of the raw power of punk honed in earlier bands to Beefheart's style of intricately shifting melodies. But Lora Logic wasn't the only woman inspired by the wilderness of Beefheart's music.

Another such individual inhabiting a wilderness was Polly Jean Harvey. Born in England the year *Trout Mask* was released, she taught herself guitar by listening to her parents' Beefheart albums. When she recorded her debut *Dry* in 1992, she integrated the primal charge of punk with the raw texture of the blues. With a wry humour, like Beefheart, she savaged pop convention with a frankness that set her apart from the more self-conscious brooding of Sinead O'Connor.

One of the more obvious figures drinking from the pond is Tom Waits. Ironically, once signed to Zappa's Bizarre/ Straight label (even touring with Zappa in the early 70s), Waits began as a melancholic singer/songwriter sitting at the piano bellowing heartache and longing like Hoagy Carmichael reborn as a beatnik. With a raspy growl, Waits spent the 70s depicting the lives of hipster lowlifes in songs like "Bad Liver and a Broken Heart" and "Heartattack and Vine." In 1983, he moved from Asylum Records to Island, after firing his manager and his producer, then dramatically changed his recording approach with *Swordfishtrombones*. His new songs ("Underground," "16 Shells from a Thirty-Ought Six") took on the shape of soundscapes, abstract short stories in which even his voice became part of the grain of the piece. An existential Harry Parch, Waits would include (among the standard bass guitars, pianos, and drums) utilitarian devices like brake drums, metal aunglongs, and buzz saws. He incorporated the rough surface of Beefheart's music without surrendering to its primal power.

As highly imaginative and riveting as Waits's music is, it is still the music of a very sane man playing the abstract artist. When Waits became a movie actor in the 80s, he learned how to vary the role-playing he exhibited too narrowly in his hipster persona of the 70s. On later records, *Rain Dogs* (1985), *Frank's Wild Years* (1987), and the terrific *Mule Variations* (1999), he remade the blues and gospel with the same sonic eclecticism Beefheart put into *Trout Mask Replica*. But he did so by acting the part of a different fish rather than becoming one. Which is why Tom Waits, as wonderfully innovative as he is, won't scare people away from their stereos.

There are many other contemporary groups that have tried to unlock the mystery of *Trout Mask*'s power and replicate it. "Frownland" was covered by the underground post-punk Scottish band Nectarine No. 9 on their 1994 album *Guitar Thieves*. Drawing from the well of free jazz and Beat poetry, Nectarine No. 9 is a musical hybrid of Albert Ayler and Vic Godard & the Subway Sect. "Frownland" also inspired the five-piece Seattle band of the same name (their latest CD, slyly incorporating Dylan, was *Sad Eyed Lady of the Frownlands*). Mixing droning guitars with Patrice Tullai's airy vocals, Frownland provides what one writer described as "melancholic elegance." Former Mothers' drummer Jimmy Carl Black and singer Eugene Chadbourne went on to form a band called Pachuco Cadaver. On CD and in concert, they covered a range of Zappa and Beefheart material (including an epic interpretation of "Veteran's Day Poppy"). A rock group soon popped up in Detroit called Bill's Corpse, a five-piece band with two drummers. Another five-piece group calling themselves Sweet Sweet Bulbs emerged out of the Big Wheel Blues Festival as a distinctive cover band doing the dark repertoire of Cowboy Junkies, John Martyn, and Nick Cave. "We are more motivational than an Anthony Robbins lecture," they reminded us with a dark chuckle.

"Dali's Car" inspired the name of the short-lived 1984 band formed by the vocalist and lyricist Peter Murphy of Bauhaus and bassist Mick Karn of Japan. The duo recorded one record, *The Waking Hour*, that included the aptly titled single "The Judgement is the Mirror." The record, as a collection of keyboard- and bass-driven songs, was a commercial disaster. Part of the problem lay in the discontentment of their collaboration. Unlike the Magic Band, Murphy and Karn had not spent time together writing or recording the songs. They preferred to send the tapes back and forth. In fact, most of the tunes were written before they came together in the studio. When they did show up together, they clashed so often that neither wanted to work together again. "Situations full of tension can often be the most creative," Mick Karn remarked echoing the underpinnings that shaped *Trout Mask Replica*. "Perhaps due to our strong, opposing opinions, there's a certain strength to Dali's Car. I doubt if there will be a reunion." There wasn't.

Other bands would turn up calling themselves Ant Man Bee or Ella Guru, some lasting, others luxuriating in obscurity like some secret society. But there were other established groups who preferred to cover the music itself. In 2000, the White Stripes would release a CD EP called *Party of Special Things to Do*, a three-song tribute to Beefheart, which included a rousing rendition of "China Pig." The punk band Dead Kennedys would do their own pulsing version of "Orange Claw Hammer." In 2003, a tribute album called *Neon Meate Dream of a Octafish* appeared (appropriately enough) on

Animal World Recordings. Beside a scattering of songs from across Beefheart's career, *Trout Mask* is well represented by A Warm Palindrome's sharp interpretation of "Orange Claw Hammer." Miss Murgatroid gives a sonic splendour to the title track, understanding the song's roots in sound poetry. Truman's Water does a lively punk version of "Hair Pie: Bake 2," while 25 Suaves take a thrash metal approach to "Dachau Blues."

For those who are under the misconception that only men listen to Beefheart, a tribute CD called *Mama Kangaroos: Woman of Philadelphia Sing Captain Beefheart* appeared in 2005. The album featured twenty female bands from Philly giving a whole new interpretation to songs like "Well" and "Orange Claw Hammer." Gary Lucas, who joined the Magic Band in the 80s, said the music ranged from "old timey to camp cabaret to bloozy rawk 'n' roll." Lucas would start his own tribute band called Fast 'n' Bulbous, making its first appearance at the Jazz en Agosto Festival in Lisbon, Portugal, on August 13, 2005. The group's purpose was to take Beefheart's music as a vehicle for both improvisation and arranging. Taking the place of Beefheart's booming voice was a four-piece horn section.

Music wasn't the only area infiltrated by *Trout Mask*. In 1997, novelist Robert Rankin wrote an absurdist autobiography titled *Sprout Mask Replica*. The front jacket is a facsimile of the album cover, featuring a man in a fedora with a sprout face wearing a suit and tie with slogan buttons all over his jacket. The book is an elliptical tale filled with short anecdotes about Rankin's mythical ancestors. While one group, the Crombies, eats metal, Rankin himself is portrayed as a man with the power of a chaos butterfly (an insect of transformation out of "Pena"). Like Beefheart's record, Rankin isn't interested in telling a formal story. The narrative is told through many threads, some leading down paranoid trails to conspiracy theories. Rankin draws inspiration from the record by making the characters aware that they are in a book, just as Zappa and Beefheart consistently made the listeners aware that they were listening to a record. For an album that few people cared to listen to in 1969, *Trout Mask Replica* was finding its way, like a termite through wood, into the unconsciousness of the culture at large.

* * *

Over the years, while others were happily drinking from the same pond, the man who created it was getting no such sustenance. Paranoia was always a lethal fuel in the air. After *Trout Mask Replica* was released, Beefheart began unleashing hostility toward John French. It took root back when the group was still working on the record. Victor Hayden had invited Jeff Bruchell, a friend, to the house to watch the band rehearsals. "Don and Jeff would observe me practising for *Trout Mask* and Jeff would say, 'I would love to do that,'" French recalled. "Don would say loudly enough for me to hear, 'Yeah, and I bet you could, too.'" Not long after the album was finished, Bruchell was suddenly sitting in with the group and French was asked to "take a walk." French did just that. He went to Wyoming to work on a cattle ranch only to soon discover, upon the album's release, that he wasn't credited on the record —despite all his invaluable contributions. (The CD has since corrected the historic revisionism.)

His departure wasn't long lasting though. In the fall of

1969, Bruchell and Jeff Cotton got into an ugly fight leading to Cotton suffering some broken ribs. By this time, Cotton had enough and left the group. But it wasn't just the broken bones that prompted his departure, it was Beefheart's consistent behaviour of railing against the group. Bruchell also abandoned ship, leaving Bill Harkleroad as the new music director. In the spring of 1970, French was invited back into the group. Upon arriving, he discovered that Beefheart had hired Art Tripp, Zappa's former percussionist in the Mothers. Tripp introduced the marimba to the group (his instrument of choice in the Mothers of Invention); French strolled right back to his drum kit. Once more, French picked up the practice of transcribing Beefheart's whistling and humming for the group's follow up album, *Lick My Decals Off, Baby* (1970). Initially, Dick Kunc was involved engineering the album. After making one small suggestion, though, Beefheart smelled betrayal. Kunc was fired, never to return. The record itself was a more refined version of *Trout Mask*, with Tripp's marimba providing contrapuntal swing to contrast to French's polyphonic drumming.

After completing the production on *Trout Mask*, Zappa was finishing up his second solo album, *Hot Rats*, which was largely an instrumental record. He had Beefheart sing the epic blues song "Willie the Pimp." In the fall of 1969, before John French returned, Zappa served as road manager for Captain Beefheart & the Magic Band when they attended the Amougies Pop Festival in Belgium to perform alongside the Soft Machine, Pink Floyd, and jazz saxophonist Archie Shepp. When they returned, Beefheart followed up *Lick My Decals Off, Baby* with the dirgelike *The Spotlight Kid* (1972). It was while working on *Clear Spot* later in 1972 that Beefheart decided to unload his barrage of invective on Zappa. Was it jealousy? Perhaps. Zappa was about to launch another record label called DiscReet, after Bizarre/Straight was dropped by Warner Brothers. Where Zappa's notoriety was growing in the 70s, Beefheart was becoming a cult figure. The hard work the group put into the radiant *Clear Spot*, which was a streamlined version of Beefheart's music (without losing any of its shimmering beauty), was a commercial disappointment, charting at number 191.

Now desperate, Beefheart started an ill-advised attempt to go commercial. He signed a contract with Mercury Records in 1974 (Virgin in the UK), with a manager, Andy DiMartino, programming him to sell out. Beefheart's first album on Mercury was *Unconditionally Guaranteed*, a record bereft of any magic. Featuring conventional jazz/pop arrangements, Beefheart's growling voice was buried in the mix. The cover art was as hopeless as the music: Beefheart eagerly grabbing a fistful of money. Did he really believe that he'd finally hit the big time? Beefheart sounded anything but big; his attempt to be a common pop crooner made him sound ridiculously fake. *Unconditionally Guaranteed* charted even worse than *Clear Spot*. The original Magic Band members were naturally appalled. They decided immediately to leave the group. At which point, Beefheart's audience started to abandon him as well, which made him angrier. When challenged, he would tell everyone that he had a right to win a Grammy. The different fish now wanted to be a common trout.

Unconditionally Guaranteed was followed by *Bluejeans & Moonbeams* (1974), another lacklustre effort with an anonymous studio band backing him. With his career almost over, he once again contacted Frank Zappa. After apologizing for all the insults, Beefheart was asked if he wanted to join the fall rehearsals for Zappa's band. He showed up just before the group's Halloween shows, but he flunked the audition because he couldn't fit into Zappa's airtight rhythm section. By the spring of 1975, though, Beefheart found his rhythm and nailed a spot in the band before their first gig at Pomona College in Claremont on April 11th. He toured the US with the group for the entire spring. When the band arrived in Austin, Texas, at the Armadillo for two nights, on May 20 and 21, 1975, they recorded what was to be the next Zappa album, *Bongo Fury*. It became something of a collaboration. *Bongo Fury* was basically an affectionate and humorous memoir about their early friendship. They traded songs and anecdotes and exchanged experiences. Without ever once getting maudlin, they reminisced about their early days in Lancaster. But it was shortlived. *Bongo Fury* would be the last collaboration between Zappa and Beefheart.

Although Captain Beefheart's career was once again revitalized thanks to the *Bongo Fury* tour, his next album, *Bat Chain Puller*, would become a casualty of a vicious lawsuit between Zappa and his former manager, Herb Cohen. Beefheart's record was initially to be released on Zappa's DiscReet label. In talking to the press, Zappa considered *Bat Chain Puller* to be "[Beefheart's] best album since *Trout Mask Replica*." Once again, Beefheart had found his true voice. But after getting caught in the legal crossfire, *Bat Chain Puller* was never issued (although some songs would be rerecorded and put out on Beefheart's next three albums on Virgin). The clash, though, brought on the final falling-out between Zappa and Beefheart. When Zappa eventually gained possession of the *Bat Chain Puller* tapes from Cohen in 1982, Beefheart and

Magic Band guitarist Gary Lucas visited Zappa with the intent of using outtakes from that session to fill out Beefheart's latest album, *Ice Cream for Crow*.

According to Lucas, Zappa had changed his mind about handing over the tapes. He told Lucas that he thought there might be a higher market in "Beefheartland" if the set was left intact. Zappa instead offered a song from the *Bongo Fury* tour, written by Zappa but sung by Beefheart, called "The Torture Never Stops." While Lucas tried in vain to negotiate with Zappa, a depressed Beefheart started accompanying their arguing with his sarcastic poem about the record business, called "There Ain't No Santa Claus on the Evening Stage." Lucas ultimately refused "The Torture Never Stops," but the torture didn't end. Zappa abruptly concluded the conversation, went back to work, and he never worked with Beefheart again. Not long after the release of *Ice Cream for Crow* in 1982, Beefheart had had enough of recording. He decided to retire from the music business. Exhausted from living out a desert island of the mind, he soon retreated to a real one, with his wife Jan, to live in a trailer and paint. There would be occasional art shows throughout the United States, but there would be no more songs from the Captain.

As for the personal dispute between him and Zappa, it finally did reach a resolution in 1993, while Zappa was dying of prostate cancer. If their friendship had begun with some harmless musical mischief at the expense of a Webcor reel-to-reel, it had been the business of music that tore them apart. Not surprisingly, music would once again become a connecting link between these two iconoclasts in the end. I read somewhere that, in their final conversation, it wasn't apologies or regrets that were exchanged. After all, what words could heal—or even change—the polar dynamics of both men? Over the phone, they did what best friends who love music always do. They played each other their old favorite records, in the end, sharing their common language.

Despite the good music that followed *Trout Mask*, there was really nowhere further for Captain Beefheart to go. Once you break down walls and find your freedom, you start to erect other walls to protect it. You end up ultimately losing the freedom you've won. None of the albums after *Trout Mask* inspired the ongoing debate that still rages over this particular record. Yet nearly forty years later, *Trout Mask Replica* is still in print, having sold to this date over 80,000 copies. But it will always be a lonely masterpiece, a record that forever carries the aura of the desert island within its grooves. As such, it will likely never inspire an intimate moment between friends, or become a touchstone for lovers. But one thing *Trout Mask* certainly isn't is negligible.

When Gertrude Stein recited what history teaches, she was taking into account that history isn't what we prefer it to be. It simply is. For some, *Trout Mask Replica* is the worst record ever made. For others, a neglected masterpiece. History records both views and backs them up. But it doesn't settle a thing. This album creates the kind of fuss that leads people to ask questions about what defines great music. It's what makes *Trout Mask* more significant than the instant and disposable pop records that dominate the charts and soon disappear.

As music, *Trout Mask Replica* will continue to resonate because it forces us to hear things that can change our way of listening. In the current turbulent political climate, it's become desirable to have our views consistently confirmed, rather than letting ourselves be truly informed. We prefer seeking security in the warm bosom of our own personal values and beliefs to expanding our ways of seeing and hearing into areas beyond personal taste. "The voice of Don Van Vliet, alias Captain Beefheart, was a signal and a proof that something else is possible—that nothing has to stay the way it is," art critic Roberto Ohrt wrote about the lasting quality of *Trout Mask Replica*. "His music came out of a space in which the power of existing laws was broken. It expanded the framework of the imaginable, for the members of a generation whose own attitudes and ideas embodied a radical aspiration, but who had let their own lives be defined by a set of descriptions and signs over which they had virtually no control."

As the 60s came to a close, there were two unrelated events that had that power to break those existing laws. I like to believe that, in some conceptual way, they mirrored each other. In the same summer month that *Trout Mask Replica* was released, a celebrated astronaut named Neil Armstrong stepped where no other man had ever walked before—on another desert island known as the moon. As Armstrong took his one small step for mankind, viewers marvelled at the brave new world unfolding before them. Meanwhile, a group of oddball musicians were about to deliver, unto an unsuspecting public, an album that just as easily could have come from Mars. Everyone drinks from the same pond indeed.

Bibliography

BOOKS

All Music Guide to Rock: The Definitive Guide, 3rd Edition (Backbeat Books, 2002).

Ball, Hugo. *Flight Out of Time* (University of California Press, 1996).

Barnes, Mike. *Captain Beefheart: The Biography* (Cooper Square Press, 2002).

Chusid, Irwin. *Songs in the Key of Z: The Curious Universe of Outsider Music* (a cappella, 2000).

Courrier, Kevin. *Dangerous Kitchen: The Subversive World of Zappa* (ECW Press, 2002).

Delville, Michel & Andrew Norris. *Frank Zappa, Captain Beefheart and the Secret History of Maximalism* (Salt Publishing, 2005).

James, Billy. *Lunar Notes: Zoot Horn Rollo's Captain Beefheart Experience* (SAF Publishing, 1998/2000).

———. *Necessity Is . . . The Early Years of the Mothers of Invention* (SAF Publishing, 2001).

Lawrence, D.H. *Studies in Classic American Literature* (Penguin Paperback Edition, 1971).

Marcus, Greil, ed. *Stranded: Rock & Roll for a Desert Island* (Knopf, 1979).

———. *Ranters & Crowd Pleasers: Pop in Punk Music, 1977–92* (Doubleday, 1993).

Miles, [Barry]. *In His Own Words: Frank Zappa*, ed. by Barry Miles (Omnibus Press, 1993).

Watson, Ben. *Frank Zappa's Negative Dialectics of Poodle Play* (St. Martin's Press, 1993).

Winner, Langdon. Essay on Captain Beefheart's *Trout Mask Replica*. (see Marcus, Greil. *Stranded: Rock & Roll for a Desert Island* [Knopf, 1979]).

Zappa, Frank with Peter Occhiogrosso. *The Real Frank Zappa Book* (Poseidon Press, 1989).

ARTICLES

Bangs, Lester. "*Trout Mask Replica* review," *Rolling Stone*, July 26, 1969.

Bianchi, Paolo. "The Painting of Don Van Vliet," *Stand Up to Be Discontinued* exhibition catalogue. Brighton Museum and Art Gallery, September 3–November 3, 1994.

Boucher, Caroline. "Zappa Stole My Ideas, Says the Captain," *Disc*, March 25, 1972.

Bowman, David. "Sharps & Flats," *Salon*, June 23, 1999.

Carey, Robert. "Captain Beefheart Pulls a Hat Out of His Rabbit," *New York Rocker*, January 1979.

Carr, Roy. "Svengali Zappa and a Horrible Freak Called Beefheart," *New Musical Express*, January 1, 1973.

Coley, Bryon. "The Strangest Album Ever Sold: The Making of *Trout Mask Replica*," *Spin*, December, 1999.

Duke Alex, and Rob DeNunzio. "Our Day with Zoot Horn Rollo," *The Captain Beefheart Radar Station*, November 1997.

French, John. "Letter from John French," *Mojo*, 1994.

———. "Behind *Trout Mask*," *Resonance*, Vol. 6. No. 1, 1997.

————. "The Ultimate Out There! Album," *Mojo*, March 2005.

Froy, Steve. "The Challenge of *Trout Mask Replica*," Beefheartologist in the U.K. Internet site.

Groening, Matt. "Plastic Factory," *Mojo*, December 1993.

Harkleroad, Bill. "Zoot Horn Rollo—A Captain's Tale," *Record Collector*, April 1998.

Johnston, Graham. "Clicks and Klangs: Gender and the Avant-Garde," *Radar Station*, August 2000.

Keepnews, Peter. "Interview with Captain Beefheart," *Downbeat*, April 1981.

McKenna, Kristine. "A Crossover of a Different Color," *Los Angeles Times*, July 29, 1990.

McKnight, Connor. *Zig Zag*, February 1973.

Miller, Jim with Janet Huck. "Captain Courageous," *Newsweek*, October 20, 1980.

Ohrt, Roberto. "The Painting of Don Van Vliet," *Stand Up to Be Discontinued* exhibition catalogue. Brighton Museum and Art Gallery, September 3–November 3, 1994.

Page, Tim. "Don Van Vliet (Captain Beefheart)," *Washington Post*, December 12, 1999. (Also, collected in *Tim Page on Music: Views and Reviews* [Amadeus Press, 2002]).

Peacock, Steve. "Beefheart the Visionary," *Sounds*, January 1971.

Spencer, Neil. "Ravaged Blues on Canvas," *The Observer*, August 28, 1994.

Wald, Eliot. "Conversation with Captain Beefheart," *Oui* magazine, July 1973.

Ward, Ed. *Review of* Lick My Decals Off, Baby, *Rolling Stone*, December 10, 1970.

Winner, Langdon. "The Odyssey of Captain Beefheart," *Rolling Stone*, May 14, 1970.

Zappa Frank. In conversation with Don Menn, "The Mother of All Interviews," from *Zappa!* tribute issue from the publishers of *Keyboard* and *Guitar Magazine*, 1993.

RADIO AND TELEVISION

Captain Beefheart: Under Review. A DVD documentary (Sexy Intellectual, 2006).

Marcus, Greil. In conversation with Geoff Pevere, *Prime Time*, Canadian Broadcasting Corporation, 1993.

Zappa, Frank. In conversation with Nigel Leigh, *The Late Show Special* on BBC2, December 17, 1993.

CD LINER NOTES

Alfonso, Barry. Interviews with Captain Beefheart, Bill Harkleroad and John French included in liner notes for *The Dust Blows Forward (An Anthology): Captain Beefheart & His Magic Band* (Rhino, 1999).

Beefheart, Captain. In conversation with Rip Rense, quoted in liner notes to the CD release of Frank Zappa's *The Lost Episodes* (Rykodisc, 1996).

Cooder, Ry. Liner notes of CD release, *A Carrot Is as Close as a Rabbit Gets to a Diamond* (Virgin Universal, 1993).

French, John. "There Ain't No Santa Claus on the Evenin' Stage," liner notes to CD box-set, *Grow Fins: Captain Beefheart & His Magic Band: Rarities [1965-1982]* (Revenant, 1999).

Also available in the series